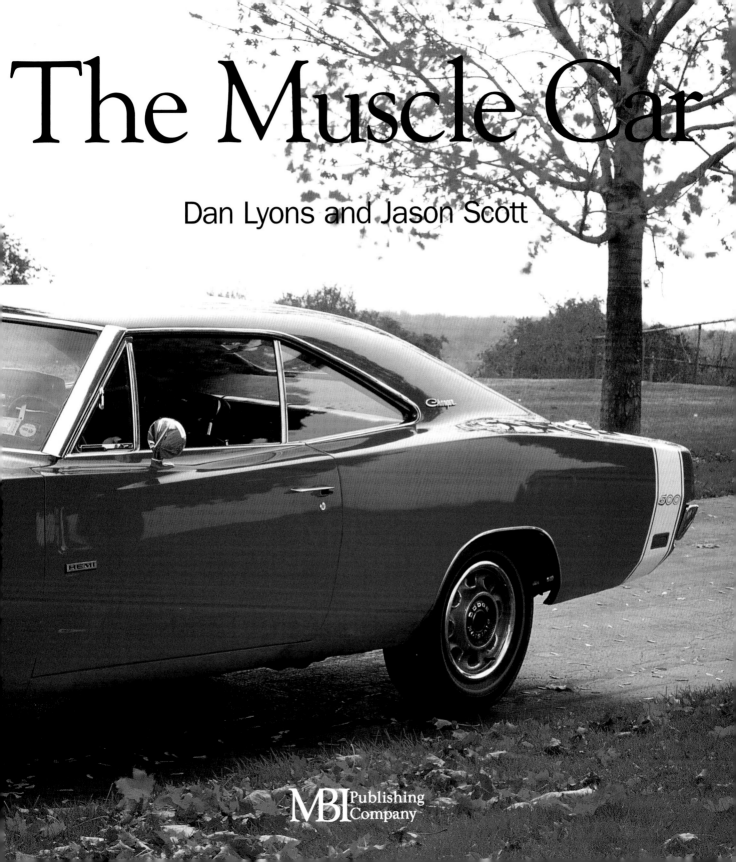

The Muscle Car

Dan Lyons and Jason Scott

MBI Publishing Company

This edition published in 2002 by MBI Publishing Company, Galtier Plaza, Suite 200, 380 Jackson Street, St. Paul, MN 55101-3885 USA

MBI Publishing Company books are also available at discounts in bulk quantity for industrial or sales-promotional use. For details write to Special Sales Manager at Motorbooks International Wholesalers & Distributors, Galtier Plaza, Suite 200, 380 Jackson Street, St. Paul, MN 55101-3885 USA.

Library of Congress Cataloging-in-Publication Data Available

ISBN 0-7603-1388-1

Printed in China

CONTENTS

INTRODUCTION

American musclecars were once plentiful and abundant, like many of the world's once-great creatures. But it's been 30 years since most of the vintage musclecars were produced, and while they're hardly extinct now, they are an endangered species. Time, traffic accidents, rising fuel costs, and even governmental legislation are all working against our beloved musclecars.

Layed out on the pages that follow are some of the most intriguing musclecars ever produced. But the intention of this book isn't to be the definitive work on "the ultimate musclecars of all time"—that's a subject far too debatable for the various GM, Ford, Mopar, and AMC fans to find much agreement on. Instead, what this book was designed to do is to help preserve the memory of some of the cars that shaped automotive history, that altered how we thought about our cars, and that changed people's lives.

Like any "best of" list, we were forced to make some hard decisions about which cars to include, about which cars were "milestone" material. A car didn't have to be ultra-rare to be worthy of inclusion; nor did it have to be ultrapopular. Most of the vehicles you'll find on the following pages are from some-

where in between those two extremes. Some may have been almost entirely overlooked in comparison to other offerings at the time, but each has its own special characteristics or traits that earned it milestone status.

Cars such as the 1964 Pontiac GTO and the 1965 Mustang are obvious choices for any milestone compilation. The 1971 Plymouth Road Runner, however, is far less obvious yet played an important role in the evolution of the musclecar. And the 1969 AMC AMX made the cut because it helped (if only for a while) save an entire car company from an untimely demise.

This book is about the dedication and against-all-odds spirit that put some of the roughest, toughest musclecars in the hands of enthusiastic buyers who appreciated brute force over creature comforts.

Ultimately, we hope you enjoy reading about these memorable musclecars as much as we enjoyed reliving old memories and putting them down in photos and words for you.

—Dan Lyons
—Jason Scott

The 1970 Shelby GT-500 was the last of a great breed of musclecar. Fitted with a 335-horsepower 428-ci V-8, this wickedly fast musclecar was one of the fastest of the era.

CHAPTER 1

General Motors

Charge of the High-Performance Brigade

There's a saying that you should "lead, follow, or get out of the way." At the beginning of the 1960s, the Pontiac Motor Division of General Motors was a follower, both in the showrooms and on race tracks. Pontiacs were excellent vehicles, to be sure, but they weren't particularly exceptional.

When John Z. DeLorean was placed in the division's highest post, as general manager, he began a rapid transformation that would put Pontiac in a leadership position and leave its sister divisions and other manufacturers scrambling to catch up.

DeLorean was quick to realize that the booming youth market wasn't satisfied with the cars that had pleased their parents during the previous decade. These younger buyers wanted smaller, sportier cars with contemporary styling. And they wanted better performance—especially the male buyers.

A young advertising executive assigned to Pontiac's account, Jim Wangers, pointed out to DeLorean that all the company had to do to attract the young, male buyers was to do for them what they had been doing on their own for years: swapping big-car engines into smaller cars to achieve a better power-to-weight ratio.

Wangers pitched a concept to DeLorean that called for installing Pontiac's 389 V-8 into the midsize LeMans/Tempest. Wangers called the car the "GTO," after the famous Ferrari of the same name. The project required little investment—after all, the company already made all the components except the emblems—and DeLorean gave it an immediate green light. And in doing so, Pontiac created the musclecar.

When the GTO debuted in the fall of 1963 as a 1964 model, it was—as Wangers had predicted—an immediate success. Combining the potent 389 (which came standard with 325 horses, but could be had with 348 with a trick-looking trio of two-barrel carbs) with the LeMans' handsome good looks was

Musclecar enthusiasts generally credit Pontiac's 1964 as the first musclecar. It was the first mass-produced car to follow the old hot rodder's practice: stuff a big engine into a small car and go win some races.

9

just the thing to get a young man's heart racing—especially when you factored in such hot-rodding mainstays as red-stripe tires, a Hurst shifter, dual exhaust, and other performance parts.

And by pricing the GTO affordably, Pontiac convinced many buyers that it was easier to buy a finished GTO off the showroom floor than to invest comparable dollars, *plus* a lot of time and effort, into building up their own older car.

The GTO was, quite simply, the right car, with the right stuff, for the right price, at the right time. But Pontiac knew how quickly buyers' interests change.

As exciting and successful as the original GTO was, it wasn't for everyone—nor was it an all-around success for Pontiac, which realized relatively little profit from the often stripped-down cars. And while part of the appeal of the original GTO was its barebones, not-included-unless-it-improves-performance nature, a few years later, when buyers of those original models got around to trading them in for new models, most had progressed to a point in life where creature comforts and image were at least as important as performance.

Not to worry—Pontiac was still ahead of the game. In 1969 it introduced a special GTO named "the Judge," which bolstered the car's image with attention-grabbing paint and graphic treatments. Though the Judge wasn't an immediate success, it made an indelible mark on the buying public's mind. A stripped-down musclecar no longer captured the younger driver's imagination. Now buyers wanted to take the wheel of a vehicle all onlookers would recognize as something special.

Four years later, in 1973, Pontiac would again foreshadow performance cars of the future when it redeveloped the musclecar to meet the particular challenges and needs of the day. Refining the popular Firebird line, Pontiac introduced the Super Duty Firebirds, engineered to perform on low-octane, low-lead fuels in order to meet federally mandated emissions requirements. Meanwhile, the cars' handling and braking were improved to broaden the overall performance "envelope." The Super Duty Firebirds—still plenty powerful—were much more politically and environmentally correct than any musclecar before

them, and set the course that all successors would have to follow.

No other manufacturer was as adaptable—let alone as insightful—as Pontiac at building musclecars. And no other manufacturer had as much impact on shaping the musclecar era.

1964 Pontiac GTO

In 1962, cars such as the Chevrolet Impala SS 409, Chrysler 300, and Ford Galaxie 500 all offered big V-8s in a two-door sedan. But those cars were not big sellers because they appealed to a maturing market. Although this group was still interested in high performance, they had other priorities on their mind, including house payments, raising kids, and being a responsible spouse. These buyers would sit in the SS 409 for a moment of dreaming—then drive away in the plain-Jane Impala.

America's youth market, however, was booming thanks to a postwar population bulge that began reaching driving age in the early 1960s. Devoid of adult responsibilities, younger buyers were free to pursue whatever struck their fancy. For teenage and

1964 Pontiac GTO

Specifications

Body	Base Price	Units Built
Coupe	$2,852	7,384
Htp.	$2,963	18,422
Conv.	$3,081	6,644
Total		*32,450*

Engine

325-hp 389-ci 4-bbl. V-8
348-hp 389-ci 6-bbl. V-8

1/4-mile (typical)

	15.5 secs.
Speed	91 mph

The GTO's "big engine" was a 389 Pontiac V-8 equipped with a trio of two-barrel Rochester carbs. With a hot cam and dual exhaust, the engine put out 348 horsepower! Most stock 1964 GTOs were fast enough to turn quarter-mile times in the high 14- or low 15-second range.

The GTO was reasonably well appointed with performance equipment inside and out. Externally, it had dual exhaust, red-stripe tires, and the mark of distinctiion—GTO emblems.

twenty-something American males, that meant one thing: performance.

This crowd, who had grown up during the days of hot rodding, knew that as fast as the full-size muscle machines were, smaller, lighter cars with the same engines would deliver better performance. And more than a few kids took it upon themselves to create those kinds of cars.

Fortunately, Detroit wasn't asleep at the wheel. The automakers took note of the small car/big engine movement that was growing in popularity, and it responded. Pontiac was first out of the gate, due to the tireless efforts of marketing exec Jim Wangers and support from the very top of Pontiac's food chain, president John Z. DeLorean. Wangers sold DeLorean on the concept of dropping the full-size Pontiac's high-output 389 into the midsize Tempest, and throwing in the usual assortment of performance amenities young buyers were likely to want or add— a floor-shifted four-speed manual transmission (or optional automatic), dual exhaust, twin-scooped hood, and other assorted goodies.

The swap was straightforward from a manufacturing standpoint, given that the 389 featured the same external dimensions as the 326 that was readily available in the Tempest. And as the young hot rodders knew, shedding weight was as effective as adding power when it came to acceleration contests.

Wangers and DeLorean settled on the name "GTO," which they pilfered from the race-winning Ferrari of the day, the "Grand Tourismo Omologato" — Italian-speak for a car approved by the FIA sanctioning body for Grand Touring competition.

Of course, Pontiac's GTO wasn't exactly designed to compete with its Ferrari namesake— though one popular magazine of the day did arrange just such a shootout and picked the Pontiac as the better bang for the buck. But where the Pontiac really shone was in stoplight-to-stoplight match-ups. And by virtue of its better power-to-weight ratio, the midsize Pontiac was more than a match for nearly any production vehicle to date, except perhaps top-optioned Corvettes.

Even in the hands of amateur drivers, the GTO was capable of low-15-second quarter-mile trips right off the showroom floor. And with minimal tuning and preparation effort, 14-second dashes were doable—all for a price that was well within the grasp of any red-blooded American boy or girl.

The GTO's combination of price, performance, and dynamite styling proved irresistible with the buying public: 32,450 GTOs were sold in 1964. Far more important than its end-of-year tally, however, was the GTO's impact on the automotive industry and performance enthusiasts. It ushered in the musclecar era and kicked off a horsepower war that would last for nearly a decade.

In the end, the 1964 GTO became the benchmark against which all later musclecars would be compared. And that's an admirable position to be in—especially when you're as well equipped as the GTO to take on all challengers.

1970 Pontiac GTO Judge

Performance-car enthusiasts were a fickle bunch. In 1963, Pontiac introduced its GTO to rave reviews and unprecedented acceptance. The car's combination of high-performance engine, attractive midsize styling, and moderate price was exactly right for the times.

But while auto manufacturers can produce and sell thousands of low-priced cars, those aren't the cars that make for outstanding profits. Pontiac realized this earlier than most manufacturers, and so by 1969, Pontiac was working hard to reinvent the musclecar.

Ironically, this higher-profit musclecar grew out of a lower-priced little brother to the GTO, code-named "the E.T.," which was intended to compete with Plymouth's budget-priced Road Runner. As the project progressed, however, one change after another pushed the car out of the bargain basement.

Pontiac's general manager, John DeLorean, insisted that the model be a GTO, and that no GTO would come with anything less than a 400-ci engine, so the E.T.'s 350 was axed. The E.T.'s planned LeMans chrome front bumper also went back to the parts shelves, in favor of the GTO's heavier, costlier Endura rubber-coated snout. Likewise, the stripped interior—complete with rubber floormats—was deemed too sparse, so a GTO's interior supplanted

Judge interiors were comfortable places to pass sentence on other musclecars. Aside from usual GTO items, like the wood wheel and woodgrain applique, special items like the Hurst T-handle shifter made the Judge even more inviting.

1970 Pontiac GTO Judge
Specifications

Body	Base Price	Units Built
Hdtp.	$3,604	3,629
Conv.	$3,829	168
Total		3,797

Engine

Std.	366-hp 400-ci 4-bbl. V-8, (Ram Air III)
Opt.	370-hp 400-ci 4-bbl. V-8 (Ram Air IV)
	360-hp 455-ci 4-bbl. V-8 (455 H.O.)

1/4-mile (typical)

E.T.	14.4 secs.
Speed	98 mph

When Pontiac showed off the new Judge package in 1969, it reinvented the musclecar and gave enthusiasts a glimpse of the future image of high performance. The body was revised and adapted to the new 1970 sheet metal, as this 1970 Judge shows.

Though largely a styling package, the Judge's base engine was the Ram Air III 400 with 366 horsepower. Optional engines included the 370-horse Ram Air IV and the 360-horse 455.

it. By the time the changes were done, the E.T. had moved considerably upscale—and had even been renamed after a popular segment on a TV sitcom of the time: The Judge.

The initial 2,000 GTO Judges were equipped nearly identically, right down to the paint scheme: a bright-orange hue named, oddly, Carousel Red, plus bold red, yellow, and blue striping and decals. Not only was the engine not a 350, it wasn't even a base GTO's 400. The base Judge engine was the Ram Air III 400 with 366 horsepower. The only optional engine was the Ram Air IV 400, which was (under-) rated at 370 horsepower. The mill featured large, round-port cylinder heads, free-flowing cast-iron exhaust manifolds, a high-rise, two-piece aluminum intake manifold, and a large Rochester QuadraJet four-barrel carburetor.

The 1973–1974 Super Duty Firebirds had superb styling, respectable acceleration, exceptional handling, competent braking, and luxurious comfort. In essence, Pontiac yet again redefined the musclecar. The 455-ci four-barrel V-8 had a mellowed 8.0:1 compression ratio and produced 250 net horsepower at 4,000 rpm, but it was still fast.

Pontiac ultimately sold just under 7,000 Judge-equipped GTOs in 1969. Despite that disappointing unit production, the Judge returned in 1970, featuring updated sheet metal, graphics, and engines, as did "lesser" GTO models. The revised 1970 nose did away with the attractive, but complex and trouble-prone hidden headlamps of 1968–69, and used a split grille that was almost indistinguishable from the new-for-1970 Firebird beak. The new fenders, door skins, and quarter panels sported sharp creasing for a tough, chiseled look. On Judge models, the side striping was changed from 1969's long nose-to-C-pillar decals to simple "eyebrows" that were applied to the fender and quarter-panel creases over the wheel openings.

Underhood, Judge options—like those of a standard GTO—expanded with the addition of two 455-ci engines, now that GM Corporate had lifted its 400-inch engine limit for midsize car lines. Both the base 455 and the H.O. (high-output) version offered a considerable torque boost over the 400s. But the top engine for racers was still the Ram Air IV 400, which retained its laughable 370-horsepower rating. Of course, the big news in engines was about the one that got away: the Ram Air V. With massive tunnel-port heads and a completely revised bottom end, the RA-V 400 was reportedly good for over 500 horsepower with just a set of headers and a tune-up. Alas, the RA-V was only built in limited quantities for testing purposes, though a few are rumored to have escaped through GM's Service Parts Operations crate motor engine program.

Despite the Ram Air and H.O. engines, the GTO Judge was hardly a match for the Hemi Mopars, the Cobra-Jet Fords, or even GM's own LS-6 Chevelle, Stage I Buicks, and W-30 Olds 4-4-2. Still, thanks to its outstanding styling, Pontiac's GTO Judge succeeded in reinventing the musclecar, by ushering in an era when image was as important as performance.

1974 Pontiac Super Duty Firebirds

By all accounts, Pontiac had no business producing the 1973 and 1974 Super Duty Firebirds. The musclecar market was all but dead (thanks to the insurance industry, OPEC, and good ol' Uncle Sam), and GM's engineering team faced an uphill battle to convert an aging line of powertrains and vehicles for the new, government-mandated reduced-emissions output and more stringent safety standards.

Quite simply, Pontiac didn't have the brainpower to spare on creating a low-volume, gas-guzzling, emissions-belching performance machine. Moreover, the 455-ci Super Duty engine alone called for dozens of new components designed specifically for it. But Pontiac knew that musclecars weren't really dead; they weren't even dying. They were evolving. And just as it had created the musclecar nearly a decade before, Pontiac was determined to re-create it for a new era.

Interestingly enough, the Super Duty was quite aptly named, for it wasn't so much a powerhouse engine—sure, the SD-455 made 310 horsepower (down to 290 for 1974)—but rather it was engineered specifically for durability.

From its beefy four-bolt main bearing caps (on all five bulkheads), through its high-strength cast crankshaft and forged-steel connecting rods, up to its incredible, free-flowing cylinder heads, the Super Duty 455 was built from the ground up to

1974 Pontiac Super Duty Firebird

Specifications

Model	Base Price	Units Built
Formula	$4,334*	58
Trans-Am	$5,024*	943
Total		*1,001*

Engine

290-hp 455-ci 4-bbl. V-8

1/4-mile (typical)

E.T.	14.8 secs.
Speed	96 mph

* model base price plus SD-455 engine option

both produce and withstand twice its standard power output. With careful modifications and select parts replacements, the Super Duty could be massaged to generate measurably more power than it came with from the factory.

Fortunately for most buyers, what the Super Duty Firebirds came with from the factory was plenty exciting already. OK, maybe 310—or even the later 290—horsepower doesn't sound that impressive, but compared to other cars of its day, it was positively excessive. Offerings from Ford, Chrysler, and even other GM divisions boasted of power outputs that were only half to two-thirds the power of the SD-455.

More important, however, the Super Duty Firebirds proved their worth on the streets and tracks. Able to cruise down the quarter-mile in the 14-second bracket, Super Duty Firebirds were able to run with the best musclecars—in factory trim or otherwise.

Yet climbing inside a Super Duty Firebird was—as with any Firebird—a delightful experience for the senses matched by few other musclecars. The bucket seats provided a comfortable, supportive position from which to grasp the sports steering wheel and the floor-mounted shifter—controlling either a Turbo Hydramatic 400 automatic or a close-ratio Muncie four-speed manual transmission. A raft of gauges in the engine-turned instrument panel allowed you to remain well informed about the health of the vehicle—and to whatever jeopardy you might choose to subject your license.

Whether Pontiac's engineers knew it or not, with the Super Duty Firebirds the company was showing the world that performance could coincide with safety, environmental responsibility, and even economy. The Super Duty Firebirds were, at once, the last hurrah for the musclecar era that was, and the first of a new breed of modern musclecars that were yet to be.

CHEVROLET: A REPUTATION BUILT ON HIGH PERFORMANCE

Chevrolet had a lot going for it during the musclecar era. It had the Chevelle, Camaro, Chevy II/Nova, and, of course, the Corvette. It had such exceptional engines as the L78 396 and L72 427 big-blocks plus a host of potent small-blocks, highlighted by the LT-1 350. It certainly had the marketing to let the public know about its cars. And then there was that little issue of price: as General Motors' "entry-level" division, Chevrolets were priced to sell—even the high-performance models and options. The beauty

The Super Duty 455 engine was a transitional engine, and it demonstrated that traditional musclecar engines could be updated with then-modern technology to produce excellent power and reduced emissions.

The 1974 Super Duty Trans-Am featured one of the most comfortable and functional muscle car interiors. High back bucket seats featured solid foam with integral springs. The Rally Gauge cluster contained speedometer, engine temperature, oil pressure, voltmeter gauges, and rally clock.

of the system, for Chevrolet, was that it sold a lot of vehicles, and the more it sold, the less it could charge for them.

Chevy had something else going for it, too: history. The company's namesake, Louis Chevrolet, was a well-known racer (of Buicks) when the company was founded and Chevrolet made sure the company was very active in motorsports. By the 1950s, that involvement had grown to include NASCAR stock car racing and extensive drag racing activities. And in 1955, Chevrolet took performance to the streets with its revolutionary "small-block" V-8, a relatively lightweight and compact 265-ci powerhouse that put out as much as 190 horsepower, in special-order trim. Just two years later, the engine had evolved to 283 cubic inches and 283 horsepower when equipped with a Rochester Fuel Injection system.

The Chevy small-block V-8 became an instant hit with hot rodders. This popularity attracted the attention and efforts of such aftermarket performance parts manufacturers, as Edelbrock, Holley, Offenhauser, and others, which produced a wide array of components to improve the engine's power, durability, and appearance. Little did anyone know at the time that 50 years later, the basic small-block Chevrolet engine would not only still exist, it would be the most popular performance engine with the largest assortment of aftermarket equipment of any engine available.

In the 1960s, Chevrolet introduced the Super Sport Impala. With power coming from an overgrown, 409-ci version of Chevy's "W" motor (an unrelated precursor to the Mark IV big-blocks) putting out as much as 430 horsepower in 1963, the Impala SS was a formidable competitor on drag strips and boulevards all across America.

But Chevrolet's first "musclecar" didn't come until 1964, when the midsize Chevelle SS debuted. With a 327-ci small-block under the hood, the Chevelle SS was at a disadvantage in horsepower and torque when compared to cars such as the GTO. Chevy corrected this deficiency in 1965 with a limited run of 201 Chevelle Super Sports equipped with the Corvette's L-78 396.

Despite less power than some of its rivals, Super Sport Chevelles sold to countless thousands of power-hungry Americans throughout the 1960s and early 1970s. Add to that the sales of Camaros, Corvettes, Impalas, Biscaynes, El Caminos, Chevy IIs, and Novas and it's easy to understand how high-performance Chevys made such a strong showing on the streets and at the race track. And thanks to sneaky methods of producing "unavailable" options under the guise of "Central Office Production Orders," or COPOs, Chevy produced some of the hottest, most outlandish vehicles ever unleashed on the American public.

But by 1971, the musclecar wars were all but over, having subsided just as quickly as they began. And while Chevy had survived the wars on the streets and race tracks, no manufacturer was able to withstand the onslaught of the federal government

1962 Chevrolet Impala SS

Specifications

Body	Base Price	Units Built
Coupe	$2,722.80*	
Conv.	$2,972.80*	
Total		99,311

Engine

Std.	135-hp 235-ci 1-bbl. I-6
Opt.	170-hp 283-ci 2-bbl. V-8
	250-hp 327-ci 4-bbl. V-8
	300-hp 327-ci 4-bbl. V-8
	380-hp 409-ci 4-bbl. V-8
	409-hp 409-ci 4-bbl. V-8

1/4-mile (typical)

E.T.	14.7 secs.
Speed	96 mph

*model base price plus SS equipment option
†includes 15,019 cars equipped with 409-ci engine

The Impala SS 409 "W" engine was so inspiring that songs were written about it and races were won with it. The renowned V-8 was available with as much as 425 horsepower with dual four-barrel carbs.

The 1961–1964 Impala SS interior was comfortable and sporty, though hardly luxurious by today's standards. This 1963 model featured all-vinyl bucket seats, which weren't widely available.

and the insurance industry. Chevy continued to put up a good fight, with cars such as the Chevelle SS, Nova SS, Z28 Camaro, and the Corvette. But the Z28, 454 Corvette, and Chevelle SS all disappeared at the end of 1974 as Chevrolet quietly conceded defeat. It would be nearly 10 years before Chevrolet would again find itself in the business of building musclecars. But that's a story for another day. . . .

1962 Chevrolet Impala SS 409

Despite explosive performance improvements, 1950s automobiles are generally remembered more for their styling than whatever powerplant lay beneath their dramatic hoodlines.

By the dawn of the 1960s, however, the exciting designs of the 1950s had given way to longer, wider, and lower body styles that gave cars the appearance of being sleeker and faster. Of course, for the majority

of cars built in the early 1960s, that appearance was just that—an appearance. Under the hood, the early 1960s cars were generally powered by updated versions of the same engines that powered their 1950s ancestors, but which seldom provided the levels of performance their body designs implied.

Chevrolet's Impala Super Sport changed all that.

With the choice of an economical 327 small-block or thundering 409-ci version of the "W-motor" V-8—with as much as 425 horsepower!—the Impala SS was well equipped to prove it not only looked fast but was fast.

Though the SS package included improvements to the suspension and braking systems, plus various interior and exterior accoutrements, it was the lineup of W-motor engines that made the Impala SS legendary.

Introduced in 1958, the first W-motor displaced 348 cubic inches and pumped out 315 horsepower—more than enough to propel the two-ton Chevys of the day down the quarter-mile in 15 seconds at nearly 100 miles per hour. Attesting to the engine's exceptional design was the fact that it developed its power with only a single four-barrel carburetor, a relatively modest hydraulic camshaft, and few performance-tuned components. A welcome byproduct of the W-motor's mild-mannered engineering was its rock-solid reliability.

The 1962 Impala was available with the 409-ci W-motor that had debuted midyear in 1961. With twin Carter four-barrels sitting atop a dual-plane aluminum intake manifold, plus a high-lift, long-duration camshaft, high-domed pistons to increase compression, and unique free-flowing exhaust manifolds, the top-option 409 was capable of revving to 6,200 rpm. When put to the test on the drag strip, showroom-stock SS 409 Impalas could trip the timers in just over 15 seconds. With traditional drag racing preparation—induction and exhaust improvements

While Chevrolet's first high-performance engine was the 1955 265 "small-block," the 1962 Impala Super Sport was the company's first sedan to be packaged and marketed based on its performance merits.

and tires with more "bite"—runs in the 14-second range awaited. Chevrolet illustrated the performance possibilities by producing a limited number of lightweight 409 Impalas for competition in the NHRA's (National Hot Rod Association) Factory Experimental, or F/X, classes. With various aluminum body panels and brackets, and *sans* unnecessary items including sound deadener, radio, and heater equipment, the lightweight 1962 Impalas were exceptionally fast. And they were the predecessors of the famous 1963 Z11 Impalas, which featured even more radical weight-saving measures and a higher-output version of the 409 enlarged to 427 cubic inches—the NHRA's seven-liter limitation.

As impressive as the 1962 Impala SS 409s were, they were only marginally successful in dealers' showrooms, accounting for just 15,019 of the 1,424,008 Impalas built that year—a figure some historians attribute to the car's mismatched attributes. On the one hand, its Super Sport equipment appealed to performance enthusiasts, most of whom were among the booming youth market. On the other hand, the car's size and styling were decidedly more conservative, which made the car an easier sell to more mature buyers. Taken individually, either attribute had what was needed to attract its intended audience, but combining the options only succeeded in alienating both markets: the older buyers weren't generally interested in the performance (nor expense) of the Super Sport package, while the younger buyers were less than impressed by the body.

But the Impala SS 409 wasn't about production figures, it was about performance figures. And to that end, the model was a bona fide success, demonstrating beyond a doubt Chevrolet's ability to produce a car capable of dominating the competition both on the street and on the track.

1967 Chevelle Super Sport

The horsepower wars were well under way by the fall of 1966, as the 1967 models debuted in showrooms across the country. Would-be buyers flocked to dealerships to see the new models: Chevy's Camaro, Pontiac's Firebird, Ford's redesigned Mustang, Plymouth's Barracuda, and others.

While those models each garnered their share of sales, the traffic they drew to showrooms was perhaps equally important, because many of those shoppers wound up purchasing other models. All too often a buyer would come into the dealership lusting after one of the exciting new models, but drive home in an established model.

One of the most popular up-sells for Chevy dealers was to move customers from the 2+2 Camaro into the more practically sized Chevelle. And for buyers drawn in by Camaro's promises of power and performance, one look at a Super Sport Chevelle was enough to close the deal.

To the victor goes the spoils, and for those buyers whose victory was a 1967 Chevelle SS, the spoils included a 396-ci big-block V-8 with a minimum of 325 horsepower and a manual transmission. More adventurous buyers could select a 350-horse 396, or the top-dog 375-horse L78 396. The engines differed in terms of cylinder heads, camshafts, induction systems, pistons, crankshafts, connecting rods, and myriad smaller components.

The 325- and 350-horse 396s were inexpensive performance engines that thrived on street driving. Thanks to a hydraulic cam, cast-aluminum pistons, cast-iron intake, and Rochester QuadraJet four-barrel carburetor, the entry-level and midlevel 396s were virtually bulletproof yet powerful enough to hold their own when battling Hemi Mopars, Cobra Jet Fords, and Ram Air Pontiacs.

RPO L78—the 375-horse 396—on the other hand, was literally a purebred racing engine, based directly on the 1965 Corvette's 425-horse L78 396. The bottom end of the L78 featured a forged steel crankshaft, forged connecting rods, high-compression forged aluminum pistons, and four-bolt main bearing caps to keep everything securely in place through high-rpm (6,000 redline) activity. Farther up in the block, a solid-lifter, high-lift cam activated

Beginning in 1966, Chevy's SS-396 Chevelle brought affordable musclecar performance to the masses. The two-door hardtop went for $2,776 and the convertible was priced at $2,962. It was refined and improved as evidenced by this 1967 model.

The heart of the SS-396 Chevelle was the 396-ci Mark IV "big-block" V-8, which was available in three performance levels: 325, 350 (shown), and 375 horsepower.

Chevelle SS interiors were businesslike but comfortable with such options as vinyl-covered bucket seats, a wood steering wheel, a console, and more. The standard transmission was a fully synchronized three-speed manual transmission made by Borg-Warner.

1967 Chevrolet Chevelle SS-396

Specifications

Body

	Base Price	Units Built
Hdtp.	$2,825	
Conv.	$3,033	
Total		63,006*

Engine

Std.	325-hp 396-ci 4-bbl. V-8 (L35)
Opt.	350-hp 396-ci 4-bbl. V-8 (L34)
	375-hp 396-ci 4-bbl. V-8 (L78)

1/4-mile (typical)

E.T.	14.8 secs.
Speed	99 mph

no exact breakdown of hardtops or convertibles exists; however, it is estimated that a maximum of 29,937 SS convertibles were built

oversize pushrods to open massive, 2.19-inch intake valves. Air and fuel flowed to those valves through a 780-cfm (cubic feet per minute) Holley four-barrel, a high-rise aluminum intake, and mammoth, nonrestrictive, rectangular intake ports instead of the smaller, oval ports in the garden-variety heads.

On race tracks, L78 Chevelles could run the quarter-mile in 14 seconds all day long, while the lower-powered 396s made for slightly slower 15-second runs. But it was on the street where the Super Sport Chevelles earned the distinction of being the ultimate musclecar for the masses: they were powerful, attractive, and most important, affordable. In 1967 alone, 63,006 Super Sport–equipped Chevelles were sold, bringing the total SS Chevelle population to 293,250 since their debut in 1964.

Chevelle remained a force to be reckoned with for the rest of the musclecar era, adding to its legendary models the 427-powered 1969 COPO Chevelles and the awesome 450-horsepower LS6 454 model of 1970.

While there were and would be more powerful and more unique Chevelles, none were any more important than the 1967 models, which redefined the musclecar.

1967 Chevrolet Camaro Z28

Chevrolet moved quickly when it saw the runaway success of Ford's Mustang. Within two years, it was able to finish its own "pony car," which had been code-named "Panther" until the eve of its introduction, when the name was abruptly changed to "Camaro."

Camaro was designed from the outset to suit a wide range of buyers, from those interested in an economical-but-stylish sporty car, to drag racers and even sports car racers. With two body styles—coupe and convertible—and roughly a dozen engines (nearly any of which could be had with a variety of transmissions), a Camaro could be ordered in a mind-boggling array of configurations. And there were scores of additional options from which to choose, allowing buyers to further personalize their Camaros.

While the SS package got all the press and attention as the "performance" options for Camaro, a little-publicized and unassuming option quietly established Camaro's reputation as a world-class competitor in the Sports Car Club of America (SCCA) Trans-Am racing series.

RPO Z28, which Chevrolet labeled as a "Special Performance Package," was the company's secret weapon to compete with Carroll Shelby's GT Mustangs for the manufacturers' championship. While racers would undoubtedly make their own specific modifications, Chevrolet provided a very complete—and *capable*—performance package, right from the factory.

The Z28 Camaro's high-winding 302-inch small-block engine is often cited as the option's principal feature; yet the car's suspension,

Z28-equipped Camaros received a special race-ready 302 small-block with a 4-inch bore and 3-inch stroke, which featured an 11.0:1 compression ratio that produced 290 horsepower. A special aluminum intake manifold, a Holley 800-cfm carburetor, a solid-lifter camshaft, forged crankshaft, forged pistons, premium connecting rods, an oil pan windage tray, and dual-exhaust were the essential go-fast goodies.

1967 Chevrolet Camaro Z28
Specifications

Body	Base Price	Units Built
Coupe	$2,930.10	602
Conv.	$3,167.10	1*
Total		602

Engine

290-hp 302-ci 4-bbl. V-8

1/4-mile (typical)

E.T.	15.1 secs.
Speed	95 mph

* one Z28 convertible is believed to have been built for a GM executive; it is not counted among the "official" production figure

Chevrolet rolled out its long-awaited Mustang fighter, the Camaro, in 1967. A few months after its release, the company quietly added an RPO Z28 option that turned the car into one of the finest-handling musclecars of its day. The list of high-performance equipment is long and distinguished—front disc brakes, dual exhaust, multi-leaf rear springs, and a plethora of others.

steering, and braking system improvements were of far more significance.

Z28-equipped Camaros received higher-rate coil springs up front and beefier leaf spring packs in the rear. Re-valved shocks complemented the new springs and helped minimize unwanted body movement, as did a larger-diameter front stabilizer bar. A unique "torque arm" that was connected to the right side of the rear axle housing helped control axle "wind-up" and wheel hop under hard acceleration, while a special, fast-ratio steering box made it easier to point the front wheels in the needed direction. Putting it all to the road were 15x6-inch steel Rally wheels wearing lower-profile, wider tires. This setup provided more traction and less sidewall deflection, which allowed for more predictable handling, especially during rapid transitions.

Racers know that good braking abilities are every bit as important as having a powerhouse engine, and so did Chevrolet. Every Z28 that left the factory had front disc brakes and revised rear drum brakes. Better brakes allowed racers to drive deeper into the corners, and then use the brakes harder to shed speed to safely navigate the turn.

As important as these other features were to the Z28's on-track success, the engine stands out as one of the top-performing small-blocks in musclecar history. Ironically, the engine was one of the primary reasons RPO Z28 was so easily overlooked by buyers. At only 302 cubic inches of displacement, the engine was perceived as a puny small-block in a big-block world. Few buyers chose to believe that the engine could be powerful, especially when a trio of 396-ci big-blocks were available in the SS models—for less money.

Chevrolet developed the 302 to meet the SCCA's strict 5-liter displacement rules for the Trans-Am series. The company had small-blocks that displaced 283, 327, and 350 inches, but nothing (at the time) in the 5-liter range. But it did have the makings of a 5-liter engine, if it creatively matched components. By mating a 3-inch-stroke crankshaft from a 283 with the 4-inch bores of a 327 or 350 cylinder block, the resulting engine would produce 302 cubic inches—just under the 305-cube maximum. As a bonus, the short stroke allowed the engine to rev to the moon

with a reasonable degree of durability, which was nearly perfect for racing use. A high-lift, long-duration camshaft, high-compression forged aluminum pistons, and free-flowing heads and induction system made for 290 horsepower and 290 foot-pounds of torque. More important, the engine was an ideal starting point for a true racing engine.

Not that the Z28 wasn't race-worthy right out of the box. In fact, the Z28 was so racy in stock form that Chevy was worried about letting inexperienced drivers get their hands on one. To prevent that, Chevrolet intentionally overlooked the Z28 option in its advertising and promotional materials, and even priced the option to minimize the chance that curious shoppers would select it.

Conversely, Chevrolet did what it could to ensure that racers were well informed of the Z28's many virtues. The presentations were good enough to rack up 602 sales of Z28s in 1967, several of which went to Roger Penske's racing team for driver Mark Donahue to pilot. And pilot them Donahue did—to within an inch of nabbing the manufacturers' championship, ultimately losing to the Mustang.

The original Z28 built a reputation that has helped the Camaro withstand the test of time, surviving from those early days through more than three decades, thrilling and satisfying drivers all the while—achievements certainly deserving of milestone status.

1967 Corvette Sting Ray

The 1967 Corvette is not the car Chevrolet had in mind. The all-new third-generation Corvette was due to be released as a 1967 model, which would have cut the "midyear" Corvette's reign to just four years—1963 through 1966. But when Zora Duntov insisted the new car go back to engineering to improve its quality before launch, Chevy had to extend the Sting Ray an extra year.

It's pure irony that the resulting 1967 Corvette would be deemed by most enthusiasts to be the best of the breed.

With no time to retool, Chevy was forced to make only minor changes to the 1966 model for another year of service. Externally, stylists removed

Corvette interiors were hardly standard musclecar fare. Rich materials, such as a real teakwood steering wheel and a stylish, twin-cockpit layout, set it apart from most of the inexpensive competition.

all extraneous trim, retaining only the crossed-flags emblem at the front of the car and the "Sting Ray" emblem on the rear. Inside, similar cleanup efforts made the cockpit a more inviting place to spend time, thanks to revised bucket seats, a relocated parking brake lever, and other tweaks.

But what really made the 1967 Corvette so much more fun were the changes under the hood: in addition to a pair of 327-ci "small-blocks"—rated at 300 and 350 horsepower—were four versions of the 427 big-block.

With the 350-horse small-block, the 1967 Corvette was a fabulous sports car, nimble and light, able to slice through corners and stop on a dime, yet with ample power to outrun even many big-blocks.

To most Corvette lovers, the 427 big-block 1967 coupe is the finest of the breed. Big-blocks such as this 390-horse 427—or the three other 427s, including the mighty 430 L88—made the Corvette a fire-breather. Though the body was cleaned up for 1967, options such as the Stinger hood and sidepipes provided a tasteful, muscular image.

29

Even from the rear, the Corvette was high style. Note the center-mounted back-up lamp, and the racing-style flip-up gas cap under the crossed-flags emblem.

1967 Chevrolet Corvette

Specifications

Body	Base Price	Units Built
Coupe	$4,388.75	8,504
Conv.	$4,240.75	14,436
Total		22,940

Engine	
Std.	300-hp 327-ci 4-bbl. V-8
Opt.	350-hp 350-ci 4-bbl. V-8
	390-hp 427-ci 4-bbl. V-8
	400-hp 427-ci 3x2-bbl. V-8
	430-hp 427-ci 3x2-bbl. V-8
	435-hp 427-ci 4-bbl. V-8

1/4-mile (typical)	
ET	15.0 secs.
Speed	93 mph

Still, some buyers were willing to sacrifice a little corner-cutting capability for the 427's big-block displacement and raw horsepower. For $200 and change, you could get the RPO L36 with its 390 horsepower. Another $105 put 10 more horses under your right foot. But if you really wanted serious horsepower at your disposal, a misleading choice was yours to make: Should you spend $437 for RPO L71, with its top-rated 435 horsepower and impressive-looking triple-deuce induction system, or fork over $947 to get . . . 5 *less* horsepower? If you opted to save yourself $500 because you wanted those "extra" 5 horses, you fell right into Chevy's trap. The company really didn't want people buying RPO L88.

RPO L88 was, for all intents and purposes, a race car in street car clothing. Developing an estimated 550 horsepower, the engine was so radical that it barely idled, didn't produce enough vacuum to feed power brakes, and didn't develop peak power until well beyond a normally streetable engine speed.

Rather than tempt incapable drivers (and probably risk wrongful-death lawsuits) Chevy purposely under-rated the L88 427 to trick buyers who were looking for the highest horsepower engine into getting the more streetable L71 engine. The company wanted to give racers access to this brutal machine, but didn't want amateur speed freaks driving more car than they could handle

In a bang-for-the-buck competition, though, the 390-horse L36 was the clear leader, and a solid foundation for a formidable street or track warrior. Not surprisingly, it was the best-selling big-block option, making up nearly one-fifth of total production for the year, with more than 3,800 copies rolling off dealers' lots, and right into the history books.

1970 Chevrolet Chevelle SS 454

Large-displacement engines had always defined the musclecar, and at no time was there more displacement than in 1970.

If the musclecar wars leading up to that year could be characterized as casual name-calling, then the escalation in 1970 could only be characterized as a knock-down, drag-out, winner-take-all street fight. And one of the hardest hitters was the redesigned 1970 Chevelle SS with the optional 454-ci Mark IV big-block V-8.

While the 1970 Chevelle SS 454 did feature a redesigned body that was heralded for its clean lines, it was its radical powertrain that commanded so much attention and instantly earned the respect of any challengers.

Mind you, the Chevelle SS had already developed a reputation as one of the toughest machines on the street, thanks to the 396-ci Mark IV engines that debuted in 1965. And in 1969, Chevy quietly upped the ante with a 427-ci Corvette variant of the Mark IV, though it made the car available only to those in-the-know under a Central Office Production Order, rather than the traditional Regular Production Order system.

But the SS 454 was a whole new animal. In base LS-5 trim, buyers got the full SS treatment, but with "only" 360 horsepower. An optional LS-6 configuration upped the horses to 450. And the fact that it was

The 1970 Chevelle SS is considered the pinnacle of Chevy's musclecar era. For 1970, five V-8 engines were available for the Chevelle SS—one 350-horsepower 396, two 375-horsepower 396 engines (L78 and L89), one 360-horsepower 454, and one 450-horsepower 454 LS-6.

being made widely available to the public bordered on sheer lunacy. (With this much juice off the showroom floor, it's small wonder the insurance industry began to take notice.)

The 454 was so astounding that, despite being engineered as a cost-effective, low-performance powerplant, the engine still developed an honest 360 horsepower—more than most high-performance engines. Yet, the LS-5 made its power without a trick part, or any fancy preparation. It relied on a cast-iron crankshaft, a passenger-car block with standard two-bolt main bearing caps, cast pistons, a mild

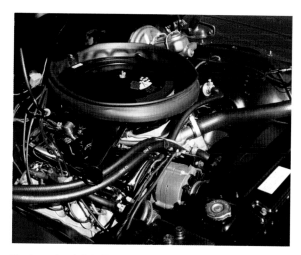

The legendary LS-6 454 Mark IV "big-block" Chevy V-8 developed 450 horsepower, featured a 11.25:1 compression ratio, and had a long-duration solid lifter cam.

Like the exterior, the 1970 Chevelle interior was all new, and perhaps the most accommodating of any musclecar. The dash contained a large analog tachometer, speedometer, and clock. Fuel, amp, and temperature gauges accompanied the mammoth three gauges.

1970 Chevrolet
Chevelle LS-6

Specifications

Body

Body	Base Price	Units Built
Coupe	$3,485.75*	
Conv.	$3,738.75*	
Total		4,475

Engine

Std.	360-hp 454-ci 4-bbl. V-8 (LS5)
Opt.	450-hp 454-ci 4-bbl. V-8 (LS6)

1/4-mile (typical)

E.T.	13.9 secs.
Speed	102 mph

*includes model base plus SS-454 (LS5) equipment, plus LS6 option price

camshaft, and low-performance oval-port cylinder heads. All were durable, low-cost parts, which helped keep the RPO Z15 SS package to a reasonable $503.45, including the LS-5, the F41 suspension system, disc brakes, and a host of interior and exterior styling touches.

The LS-6, however, was the favorite among the press, enthusiasts, and would-be buyers. For all intents and purposes, the LS-6 was a large-displacement version of the L-78 396. Chevy fitted the LS-6 with its finest high-performance pieces, such as a forged crankshaft and rods, forged aluminum 11.25:1 pistons, large-port heads, and a low-rise aluminum manifold (which was actually dictated by the Corvette's minimal hood clearance).

The second-generation Camaro was introduced with much fanfare in 1970. The fastback two-door coupe incorporated European styling trends and provided improved handling through a redesigned suspension. The track was pushed out 1.5 inches in front and 1/2 inch in back. Chevy eventually offered the F41 performance handling package that included heavy-duty shocks, a larger-diameter front anti-sway bar, and a rear anti-sway bar.

The Z28 housed what many consider to be the best small-block V-8 GM ever produced—the 350-ci LT-1 engine. Based on the Corvette engine, it featured a forged steel crankshaft, drop-forged steel connecting rods, and forged aluminum pistons.

Officially, the LS-6 developed 450 horsepower. But it was hardly a secret that manufacturers often under-rated engines in the hope that doing so would result in the car being misclassified into a lower-than-appropriate racing class. Under-rating also became a great way to win favor (or at least try to) with the insurance industry, which began cracking down on performance cars at the end of the 1960s. Independent dyno tests of stock LS-6 454s equipped with headers typically showed numbers in the neighborhood of 550 horsepower.

Ironically, the LS-6's power was, in some ways, its own worst enemy. With 500 foot-pounds of wrenching torque, the tires didn't have a prayer of maintaining traction. But that was actually a good thing. If the tires could have harnessed the LS-6's power, failures of the transmission, U-joints, and rear axle assembly would have been far more prevalent than they already were, plus would have cost Chevy a fortune in warranty repairs.

Even when the 454's torque wasn't breaking parts it was creating problems. For instance, buyers who opted for the four-speed manual transmission had to contend with shifter linkage that jammed under hard acceleration as the engine's torque caused the engine and transmission assembly to rock sideways, wedging the linkage up against the floor pan. Obviously, those who opted for the shift-for-itself Turbo 400 automatic had no such worries.

When the rest of the car was modified to properly harness the 454's power, the car ran like a tiger. An LS-6 454 Chevelle could handily dash through a quarter-mile in under 13 seconds with slicks and a good tune-up. Adding headers and swapping the low-rise intake for a more efficient high-rise unit would bump power measurably. And if you put the Chevelle on a diet (they had grown pretty hefty), quarter-mile elapsed times (E.T.s) in the 12-second range were possible at speeds well above 100 miles per hour.

For many enthusiasts, there is no greater musclecar than the 1970 LS-6 Chevelle SS 454. And certainly none is more iconic of the era of excessive power and outstanding styling.

1970 Chevrolet Camaro Z28

General Motors had established a tradition of redesigning vehicle bodies every two years. On the in-between years, it usually introduced reengineered drive trains and made other mechanical improvements. This not only kept the product line fresh and exciting to buyers each fall, it also spread out the engineering workload for GM.

But Chevrolet flip-flopped that schedule with the 1970 Camaro.

It should be understood that there was little reason to redesign the Camaro for 1970. After all, the model was only three years old, and it had been restyled for 1969 with a more aggressive appearance, requiring the redesign of every body panel except the hood and the roof. And the new look was a rousing success, judging by the record 243,085 units produced for the production run—which, by the way, was extended abruptly when the United Auto Workers went on strike, delaying the launch of the all-new 1970 model.

Likewise, the Camaro powertrains were hardly lacking. In 1969 buyers could choose from among 12 different engines: there were two six-cylinders, five small-block V-8s, and five big-blocks. Additionally, there were eight different transmissions, and an array of rear-axle gear ratios.

Chevrolet had learned that a completely new Mustang was due in 1971, when it had planned to release a redesigned Camaro. Launching a new Camaro at the same time as a new Mustang would have splintered the market: both would be "all-new," thus neither would have a clear advantage. Armed with this knowledge, Chevy decided to get the jump on its rival and release the new Camaro a year early.

The new Camaro was elegantly styled with a decidedly European look. With its long hood and short, fastbacklike rear, the 1970 F-body was reminiscent of various Jaguars, Alfa-Romeos, and Lancias. The car was long, low, and sleek, just like any good sports car should be.

Under this fresh sheet metal was a new, world-class suspension system that gave Camaro outstanding handling abilities. Large-diameter, vented front disc brakes were made standard equipment to ensure that every Camaro had braking power to match. And that was just the base model; Z28 suspension, steering, and braking systems were highly tuned for improved handling and stability at racing speeds.

On first glance, the 1970 Camaro's engine line-up appeared to take a step backward, retreating to only one six-cylinder (the 250-inch straight six), two sizes of small-blocks (307 and 350 cubes), and the

To improve rear downforce, a spoiler was attached to the deck lid; this Z28 features the "late"-style three-piece spoiler.

1970 Chevrolet Camaro Z/28

Specifications

Body	Base Price	Units Built
Coupe	$3,411.95 *	8,733
Total		8,733

Engine

360-hp 350-ci 4-bbl. V-8 (LT-1)

1/4-mile (typical)

ET	14.5 secs.
Speed	99 mph

*includes base (V-8) model plus RPO Z28 option equipment

396. Gone were the beastly 427s of 1969, and the new 454-ci big-block was notably absent from the order form. The 5-liter 302 that had been such a critical part of the Z28's introduction three years ealier was also gone.

Thanks to a rules change at the SCCA, Trans-Am competitors could now utilize 5.7-liter engines, which allowed Chevy to replace the 302 with its larger-displacement 350, in the form of the new 360-horsepower LT-1. The extra cubes provided a significant torque increase—an 80-foot-pounds jump to 370—over the twitchy 302 that had preceded it. The heartier torque curve even allowed for a welcome addition to the Z28 option list: an automatic transmission.

With its new looks, new underpinnings, and new drive train, the 1970 Camaro Z28 was, quite simply, the best Z yet, and possibly the best Z28 ever. And though the Z28 wasn't able to clinch a third straight manufacturers' championship in the Trans-Am series, it nonetheless raised the bar for all future sporty cars.

OLDSMOBILE: AN IMPECCABLE BLEND OF MUSCLE AND LUXURY

Musclecars weren't the only things racing in the 1960s. It was also the time of the "space race" between the United States and the Soviet Union.

The space race captured the attention and imagination of the world, including the marketing and engineering teams at Oldsmobile. Olds created a new logo that bore more than a passing resemblance to a rocket at liftoff. Carrying the spacecraft theme underhood, the company slapped the "Rocket" name on its high-performance engines. More important, Olds engines were given more thrust than NASA's Atlas rockets, which made it even easier to put space between your Olds and the competition. Yet unlike NASA's rocket, Oldsmobile's Rockets were tailored for comfort while others were built solely for speed.

True to Oldsmobile's prime directive, the 4-4-2 was much more than just an overpowered engine in a cheap package. The 4-4-2 offered style and comfort from the outset. With high-grade materials and judicious application of bright trim work (and later even woodgrain trim), the 4-4-2 was a civilized, dignified musclecar equally at home at a country club or a drag strip.

Such refinement would continue to be Oldsmobile's hallmark throughout the musclecar era. While other manufacturers gave relatively little concern to anything but power and performance, Oldsmobile paid attention to the details. As a result Olds produced some of the most attractive, most drivable muscle of the period.

Oldsmobile's attention to details caught the eye of high-performance shifter manufacturer George Hurst, leading to one of the most well-known and interesting alliances in automotive history.

Aside from supplying the standard high-performance shifter on more musclecars than any other company, Hurst also dabbled in creating ultra-performance super cars, much like the Yenko Chevrolets, the Royal Bobcat Pontiacs, or the Tasca Fords. Hurst built one-off ultra-customs, such as the twin-engine, four-wheel-drive Hurst Hairy Olds, which he used as promotional exhibition vehicles at drag strips across the country. But he desperately wanted to build his own line of performance vehicles. His concept was simple: an executive hot rod. Hurst wanted a car that upper management would be comfortable driving to the office Monday through Friday—in 12 seconds flat.

He approached Olds with the idea just when the division had determined that it needed an "image" car to draw buyers into the showrooms. Thus, the legendary Hurst/Olds allegiance was formed. Based on the Olds Cutlass platform—the same model as the 4-4-2—Hurst was able to provide Olds with a convenient way to skirt around some internal GM edicts, namely the 400-ci displacement limit for the intermediate-size Cutlass. Hurst contracted Olds to supply both partially assembled 4-4-2s and custom-built Toronado 455s that were set up with loose tolerances to allow the engines to make more power through decreased internal friction. Hurst then mated the engines to the cars, made a number of lesser changes, added special paint striping, and sold the cars through Olds dealers. The plan was successful, despite the fact that only about 500 cars were built.

In the years that followed, Hurst repeated the process several times, even into the 1980s.

Meanwhile, with buyers flocking to Olds showrooms to see the outrageous Hurst/Olds hot rods, the job of selling less-expensive 4-4-2s became easier and easier. By 1970, GM had rescinded its cubic-inch limit, which allowed Olds to install its 455-cube W-30 engine into 4-4-2s right on the assembly lines, thereby negating much of the need for Hurst's creations. In the process, Olds proved it could build its own executive hot rod—one that's remembered and revered to this day.

1970 Oldsmobile 4-4-2 W-30

Dr. Oldsmobile, the GM division's fictional musclecar-mad scientist, had been working hard in his laboratory throughout the 1960s producing a number of the hottest musclecars of the era. For 1970, Oldsmobile outdid himself when he concocted the new W-30 4-4-2.

While other manufacturers were busy creating stripped-down race cars for the street, the good Doctor made the 4-4-2 a best-of-both-worlds combina-

tion. Like any good musclecar, the W-30 4-4-2 had power to spare; but it also had ample amenities to keep the car comfortable for long cruises—or quarter-mile blasts.

The muscle was provided by a new 455-ci Oldsmobile V-8. In the past, GM's top brass had a 400-ci displacement limit on all of its intermediate-sized passenger cars, including the 4-4-2, the GTO, the Chevelle SS, and Buick's GS. But with the competition powered by 426 Hemis, 440 Magnums, 428 Cobra Jets, and 429 Super Cobra Jets, GM had no choice but to match motors, inch-for-inch—or better.

Olds' Rocket 455 was a strong motor to start with, and had proven itself in Olds' full-size cars for years. But in W-30 trim, the 455 benefited from a hotter camshaft, increased compression, a free-flowing intake with large Rochester QuadraJet carburetor and cold-air induction system, dual exhausts, and more. The package was rated at 370 horsepower and an earth-moving 500 foot-pounds of torque.

1970 Oldsmobile 4-4-2 W-30

Specifications

Body	Base Price	Units Built
Hol. Coupe	$3,376	
Sport Coupe	$3,312	
Conv.	$3,567	
Total		3,100*

Engine

Std.	365-hp 455-ci 4-bbl. V-8
Opt.	370-hp 455-ci 4-bbl. V-8 (W30)

1/4-mile (typical)

E.T.	14.3 secs.
Speed	100 mph

*no by-model breakdown information is available

Oldsmobile's 4-4-2 blended high performance and luxury into one solid package. In 1970, the 4-4-2's massive 455-ci engine was offered as the W-30 high-performance option that featured an aluminum intake manifold, 328-degree camshaft, and disc brakes.

With either a four-speed or heavy-duty version of the TH400 automatic, plus a Positraction-equipped heavy-duty rear axle assembly, the 4-4-2 W-30 could dash down the quarter-mile in less than 15 seconds on street tires. With better traction and a less restrictive exhaust system, the 4-4-2 W-30 was capable of dipping into the 13-second bracket—complete with its bucket seats, rich woodgrain interior

trim, and other accoutrements. Further modifications put 12-second runs within reach.

Thanks to its impressive list of performance equipment and creature comforts, the 4-4-2 W-30 was hard to beat. In fact, there was only one way Dr. Oldsmobile could top it—by *un*topping it. Whether in convertible form or the more traditional hardtop form, many enthusiasts consider the Olds 4-4-2

The W-30 was derived from a 370-horsepower version of Olds' 455-ci "Rocket" V-8, which was fed cool, outside air by the fiberglass twin scoop Ram Air that had a flapper-door air cleaner. The 1970 W-30 had dynamite looks, especially in convertible form. Note the optional red inner fender liners.

Equipped with bucket seats, woodgrain dash, and a large tachometer and speedometer, the W-30's interior was a comfortable, attractive place to pass time—or pass just about anything else on the road, especially your competition.

W-30 to be the ultimate musclecar, combining stunning good looks with a lavish interior, and an almost unbeatable powertrain.

Sadly, just 3,100 W-30 4-4-2s were produced for 1970, and by 1971, the option had become a mere shadow of its 1970 self, suffering from lower compression, milder cam timing, and other changes that robbed the W-30 package of its soul. But for one brief year, the W-30 4-4-2 was as hot an Olds as one could find, and one of the hottest, best-mannered musclecars around.

BUICK: A SYNERGY OF STYLE AND SUBSTANCE

In GM's divisional heirarchy, Buick is one step beneath Cadillac: luxury car comforts without the luxury car price tag. But beneath the company's spit-polished, squeaky-clean image lurks a rebellious spirit that craves fun and excitement.

To the uninformed, "Buick musclecar" sounds like an oxymoron, or at least a mis-statement. Yet while performance cars weren't Buick's specialty, the straightlaced division still managed to put out some of the hottest vehicles in musclecar history.

In the early 1960s, Buick made a nod toward performance with its Wildcat and Riviera. When Chevy, Olds, and Pontiac introduced their new intermediate-sized muscle machines as 1964 models, Buick held off. Its entrant into this market was another year in coming—but well worth the wait. The 1965 Skylark Gran Sport, or simply GS, was a musclecar as only Buick could make it: loaded with comfort and conveniences, and *over*loaded with power.

To stand up to its powerful peers, the Buick GS came equipped with a 401-ci Buick V-8—which somehow squeaked past GM's 400-ci displacement limit for its midsize cars. A three-speed gearbox with floor shifter, dual exhaust, heavy-duty suspension, and other goodies rounded out the package. With 325 horsepower and 445 foot-pounds of torque, the GS took off as if shot from a catapult.

Buick's conservatives insisted the car still be a Buick, which meant retaining the features that had made Buick an outstanding buy as a family car: rich upholstery, extensive conveniences, and classic styling.

The GS walked that precarious line between style and substance well—perhaps too well, as the public barely took notice. Until 1970, that is.

In 1970, Buick took out all the stops to develop the ultimate GS: the GSX.

To ensure that the GSX looked like no other Buick, the car was available in only two colors: Apollo White or Saturn Yellow. Regardless of which a buyer selected, the car received bold black striping that ran along its sides and up and across the pedestal-mounted deck lid spoiler. The GSX hood had massive black stripes separated by the hood's center crease, a tachometer mounted in a rearward-facing scooplike bubble, and twin holes that provided cold air for the induction system of the car's 455 V-8. Most GSX Buicks were fitted with the top-option Stage 1 455, though a few were built with only the 360-horse standard 455.

Like the Hurst/Olds models of 1968 and 1969, the 1970 Buick GSX was an outstanding traffic builder for Buick dealers. And the car did a lot to change the company's image, making the public realize that Buick wasn't just a stodgy old man's car. It was a car for younger drivers and performance enthusiasts, too.

Sadly, the GSX was a one-hit wonder. Though Buick offered a GSX option on cars throughout the early 1970s, only the original commands much respect or admiration among enthusiasts or collectors today. For the most part, the 1970s saw Buick retreat to its comfort zone, providing Cadillac content at Chevrolet prices.

In the 1980s, however, the company mustered a performance resurgence as America caught NASCAR fever. Buick dechromed its midsized Regal, drenched it in ominous onyx black paint, and topped it off with an unusual powerplant—a turbocharged (and later intercooled) 231-ci V-6 that produced 245 horsepower.

The Buick Regal Grand National, or GN for short, made the world take notice of Buick at a time when GM's cars were often criticized for their "cookie cutter" looks. And conservative, luxurious Buick had the distinction of producing the quickest car in America when it assembled a limited run of

300-horsepower Grand Nationals, dubbed the GNX.

So, while Buick's modern lineup doesn't offer any true performance cars, the company "for the supercharged family" may just be waiting until the time is right to unleash its next X model. And if history is any indication, a new Buick X model would be nothing short of exceptional.

1970 Buick GSX

At first glance, Buick's 1970 GSX looked like a Pontiac GTO Judge or maybe Olds' new-for-1970 Rallye 350. As with both of those models, the GSX sported bold hood and side stripes, a deck lid spoiler, and vibrant colors—Saturn Yellow or Apollo White, take your pick. And in many ways all three models were similar.

But the GSX was hardly a copycat musclecar. Buick had plenty of experience building performance cars, including its Gran Sport (the "GS" in GSX), the Wildcat, and even the Riviera, so it didn't have to "cheat" to develop a powerful performance machine.

While the performance Buicks were handily capable of running with 4-4-2s, Road Runners, and Fairlanes, Buick went to great lengths to ensure that the

1970 Buick GSX

Specifications

Body	Base Price	Units Built
Hdtp.	$4,881	678
Total		678

Engine

Std.	350-hp 455-ci 4-bbl. V-8
Opt.	360-hp 455-ci 4-bbl. V-8 (Stage I)

1/4-mile (typical)

E.T.	14.2 secs.
Speed	101 mph

Buick's Gran Sport ("GS" for short) had often been overlooked as a musclecar—until the GSX came along. The top-shelf GS featured audacious styling with Ram-Air hood and rear deck spoiler. Only 678 of these big-block monsters were built in 1970.

One of the GSX's classic features was the hood-mounted tachometer with a 5,000-rpm redline.

Buick's awesome Stage 1 455 produced 360 horsepower, which was more than enough to allow some unmusclelike options, such as air conditioning and power steering. But the big-block had stump-pulling torque as well; the 510 foot-pounds rating was one of the highest of the musclecar era.

Skylark GS lineup was always something more than just another musclecar. The boys from Flint built in a high level of comfort and convenience. Things that were either extra cost or simply unavailable on other musclecars came as standard equipment on the GS.

The GSX took that philosophy to an eXtreme, if you'll pardon the pun. It offered both more muscle and more luxury. For power, the GSX started with a 350-horse 455-ci Buick V-8—the largest V-8 ever offered in the intermediate-sized Skylark body. Buyers with an insatiable craving for power could have their 455 served up in Stage I trim, which added 10 more horsepower on paper—a figure most enthusiasts argue was grossly underrated, citing countless victories against Hemi Mopars and SS 454 Chevelles as proof that the horsepower difference was much greater than Buick let on.

The GSX's performance package also consisted of the usual musclecar goodies: a manual four-speed transmission, a 3.42:1 heavy-duty rear axle assembly with a Positraction limited-slip differential, raised-white-letter (Buick referred to them as "billboard") tires, and dual exhaust. More unique were the GSX's standard power front disc brakes, its front *and* rear anti-roll bars, the rear deck lid spoiler, and, especially, the front spoiler.

Luxury touches on the GSX included standard bucket seats, a deluxe steering wheel, special instrumentation featuring a way-cool hood tach, styled steel wheels, power steering, power brakes, and rich-looking upholstery. Plus, unlike many other musclecars, the GSX was available with a vast assortment of convenience options, including air conditioning, power windows, a variety of sound systems, and virtually any other Skylark option. Most musclecar manufacturers, by comparison, eliminated such luxuries as air conditioning on top performance options more to discourage average buyers from purchasing barely civilized cars.

Unfortunately, the local Buick dealership wasn't exactly the musclecar set's first stop when they went shopping. As a result, just 678 GSXs were produced for 1970—491 were Saturn Yellow and the remaining 187 were bathed in Apollo White. Records indicate that 400 of the cars were equipped with the top-option Stage 1 engine, meaning that the average challenger who drew up beside a 1970 GSX at a stoplight had a *very* hard time beating it to the next light.

Based on its parts and performance, the 1970 Buick GSX was considered the baddest Buick ever. Not until the limited run of 547 GNX Grand Nationals in 1987 did the division build anything hotter.

CHAPTER 2

Ford Motor Company

The Pony Car Creator

It's been said that racing improves the breed. At Ford Motor Company that saying was practically a way of life. Henry Ford realized early on that nothing demanded more from a car than a good race. And while it was inevitable that parts would break, Ford used that opportunity to improve the parts so they wouldn't break again. In doing so, Ford developed a reputation not only for building performance cars, but also for commitment to quality.

Competing publicly in races had a second benefit: exposure. The better a manufacturer did at the races, the more recognition it got from the press, and thus from car buyers and, especially, enthusiasts. In short, drawing attention at the race track could draw the public to your dealerships.

As sales soon indicated, buyers like to drive winners, not losers. So, those three factors—quality, awareness, and vanity—all had a part in the "What wins on Sunday, sells on Monday" philosophy.

In the 1950s, two forms of motorsports dominated the hearts and imaginations of automotive enthusiasts—and garnered the lion's share of "support" from auto manufacturers: stock car racing and drag racing.

Ford was a stalwart competitor in both arenas, and despite a ban that prevented any "official" involvement in motorsports by the Auto Manufacturers Association, Fords were still a regular sight on victory lane.

Moving into the 1960s, manufacturer after manufacturer gradually discontinued its support of the AMA ban, Ford included. Practically within days of publicly announcing it would no longer support the AMA antiracing actions, Ford launched its "Total Performance" campaign, one of its most successful marketing efforts ever.

More important, Ford's engineering teams were now given budgets to improve both cars and parts for competition use—in contrast to the era of the AMA ban, when such projects were carried out on shoestring budgets, if

Ford hit the jackpot with its 1964 1/2 Mustang and sold over 500,000 copies in the first year. Based on the Ford Falcon, the Mustang was just what young Americans wanted—good looks and sporty performance—at a price they could afford. The Mustang was available with a variety of engines—the 170 inline six, a 200-ci V-6, a 260 V-8, and the hi-po 289 V-8.

45

The Mustang's interior came standard with lots of items buyers typically had to pay extra for on other models, including bucket seats and a floor-mounted shifter.

money was available at all. The injection of money into the engineering departments resulted in an unprecedented increase in the number and quality of performance parts. New intake manifolds, new cylinder heads, entirely new engines, and even entirely new vehicle bodies were all designed to put Fords first on race day. And those same parts filtered onto the production lines, down to dealers' lots, and into the driveways and garages of John and Jane Q. Public.

Cars such as the slippery Torino Talladega that cheated the wind on NASCAR's high-banked super-speedways, or the 1968 1/2 428 Cobra Jet Mustangs that took the drag racing world by storm, were just two examples of how official involvement in racing led to new products—and a greatly improved performance image.

A side benefit of Ford's racing activities was a series of collaborative projects with established race shops. From its involvement with Carroll Shelby came the legendary Shelby Mustangs; work with stock car specialists Holman & Moody contributed to the development of the Boss 429 engine and other NASCAR innovations.

Many of the Fords from the Total Performance era set performance standards against which all other cars of the day are judged—milestones along the road of musclecar history.

1965 Mustang

While Pontiac's 1964 GTO marks the beginning of the musclecar era, the Ford Mustang's impact on the automotive landscape can hardly be overstated. With this model, derived from the humble Falcon, Ford created a new breed of performance automobile: the pony car.

Ford actually produced the Mustang to compete with Chevy's sporty Corvair in the sales race. Little did Ford know that the Corvair would soon be dealt a lethal blow from consumer advocate Ralph Nader, whose book, *Unsafe At Any Speed,* characterized the rear-engined sedan as a death machine. Fortunately for Ford, Mustang's platform—devised by Lee

1965 Ford Mustang

Specifications

Body

	Base Price	Units Built
Coupe	$2,320.96	501,965*
Fastback	$2,533.19	77,079
Convertible	$2,557.64	101,945*
Total		680,989

Engine

101-hp 170-ci 1-bbl. I-6 (early)
120-hp 200-ci 1-bbl. I-6
164-hp 260-ci 2-bbl. V-8 (early)
200-hp 289-ci 2-bbl. V-8
210-hp 289-ci 4-bbl. V-8 (early)
225-hp 289-ci 4-bbl. V-8
271-hp 289-ci 4-bbl. V-8 (hi-po)

¼-mile (typical)

ET 15.9 secs.
Speed 85 mph

*Includes early- and late-1965 production runs

The hi-po 289-ci engine cranked out 271 horsepower at 6,000 rpms and made the "Stang" a competent performer. The 289 featured a nodular iron crankshaft, heavy-duty connecting rods, and an oversized crankshaft balancer.

Iacocca, who would later lead Chrysler to salvation—was both sportier and safer than Corvair's.

The Mustang was safe for Ford in two ways: part vehicle design and part corporate risk-management. On the design side, Mustang did not follow the Corvair's rear-engine layout, which made it so unsafe in Nader's and the public's eyes. From a corporate standpoint, Mustang was a "safe bet," given that it was built on the same platform as the company's already successful and economical Falcon. The Mustang's budget-minded specifications also made it quite affordable.

The car's sporty character derived largely from its powerful engine lineup, which featured an exciting "hi-po" 271-horsepower 289 V-8. This motor was added to the option list in June 1964, just a few months after the model's April 17 introduction. With the hi-po 289 and a four-speed, the new pony car was a fast runner even among big-block competition.

Ford hit the mark with more than just the car's layout and performance. Mustang's stylish body, intentionally designed with a European flair, proved to be enticing to young American men and women. To ensure there was a Mustang for nearly any buyer's needs, Ford designers fashioned the key styling elements into three Mustang bodies: a coupe version, a fastback model, and a convertible.

Calling the Mustang anything short of a grand-slam sales success would be a gross injustice. More than 680,000 Mustangs were assembled for model year 1965, combining both 1964-1/2 and 1965 production figures. Only a small percentage of these cars were built with the hi-po 289. Most rolled off the assembly lines with either a 170-ci straight-six or 260-ci V-8—hardly brutal performers, but clearly satisfactory to a huge number of buyers.

Having stormed the market with the initial Mustang, Ford evolved the model along the trend toward bigger engines and greater horsepower. In the years to come, some of the most astounding musclecars would bear Ford's famous galloping-horse emblem, including the Cobra Jet Mach 1, the Boss 302, and the mighty Boss 429. These formidable descendents reinforce the 1965 Mustang's place in musclecar history.

1966 Shelby Mustang GT-350

From the moment the Mustang debuted, enthusiasts recognized its performance potential. The 260-ci

1966 Shelby GT 350H Mustang

Specifications

Body	Base Price	Units Built
Fastback	$4,428	1,000
Total		*1,000*

Engine

306-hp 289-ci 4-bbl. V-8

1/4-mile (typical)

	14.7 secs.
Speed	92 mph

Shelby interiors offered few creature comforts, but improved on base Mustang innards with a wooden three-spoke steering wheel plus a tachometer centered on the top of the instrument panel.

Shelby GT-350 Mustangs—including the GT-350H Hertz model—featured shock-tower and LeMans ("export") braces to strengthen the chassis. The engine was a modified version of the hi-po 289 that pumped out 306 horsepower.

V-8, available when the car was introduced, was not a fire-breather itself, but a sign of what was possible, and hopefully forthcoming.

Naturally, Ford could have built a souped-up Mustang on its own, but the company had all it could do to keep up with demand for the models already available. Besides, the company knew that the quickest way to develop a reputation of winning performance was to actually make winning performances. And what better way to accomplish that than by having a real race team build a race car out of a Mustang?

Ford already had a relationship with Carroll Shelby, who stuffed Ford drive trains into British two-seaters. Shelby called the cars Cobras, but the

Ford contracted Carroll Shelby to build special racing versions of the Mustang fastback called the GT-350. In turn, Shelby built 1,000 GT-350s for the Hertz rental car company that received the "H" designation. The cars featured black paint, gold striping, and Magnum 500 wheels.

competition called them bad news. With their small size, light weight, and abundance of power, the Cobras were ferocious on race courses and almost unbeatable.

Because of the reputation Shelby had developed building and racing Cobras, Ford logically concluded that a car with Shelby's name would get lots of attention at dealerships and on the streets. Ford approached Shelby about the idea and the rest, as they say, is history.

The first Shelby Mustangs, the 1965 models, were built at Shelby-American's airplane-hanger-turned-assembly-plant in California. Ford shipped semifinished fastback Mustangs to Shelby to be completed. The cars, as supplied by Ford, lacked hoods, back seats, exhaust systems, and emblems. And while the cars were equipped with Ford's top-of-the-performance-line powertrains—including the 271-horse 289 V-8, a Borg-Warner four-speed, and a 9-inch Detroit Locker rear axle assembly outfitted with oversized station wagon brakes—Shelby and company made numerous modifications to raise the cars to within a whisker of true racing specs.

The engines were outfitted with a high-rise aluminum intake manifold, Holley four-barrel carburetor, equal-length tubular exhaust headers, and some dress-up goodies such as the finned-aluminum Cobra valve covers. The upgrades added some 35 horsepower. To make sure that power could be put to use consistently, Shelby's team redesigned the suspension to improve the car's stability in corners. The front suspension geometry was radically altered, and new springs were installed that dropped the front end by roughly an inch. An oversized anti-roll bar helped keep the car level in the curves, while Koni shocks at all four corners kept the wheel movements under control.

By the time Shelby finished with the cars, the Shelby GT-350 Mustangs—and especially the competition version, the GT-350R—were about as close to real race cars as you could get on the streets, and about as far removed from stock Mustangs as imaginable. Too far, in fact, for Ford's taste.

Shelby was instructed to "civilize" the GT-350 for 1966, which he did—but just barely. He added air conditioning to the option sheet, along with a heavy-duty version of the C-4 three-speed automatic. In addition, the 1966 Shelby was available in six colors, which starkly contrasted with the Wimbledon White–only 1965s. Buyers responded favorably to the 1966 Shelby Mustangs, including Hertz Rent-a-Car, which put in an order for 1,000 Shelby Mustangs in special black paint with gold stripes and accents. At year's end, more than 2,200 Shelby Mustangs had been assembled.

Unfortunately, later Shelby Mustangs were gradually watered down into more Mustang and less Shelby, as Ford's control over production increased and Shelby's interest in the Mustang market waned. But it was the Shelby GT-350 that established the Mustang as a true performance machine, with plenty of wins to prove it.

1969 Ford Mustang Mach 1

When America entered the jet aircraft age in the 1950s, the buzz was all about going faster, going

1969 Ford Mustang Mach 1
Specifications

Body	Base Price	Units Built
Fastback	$3,122	72,458
Total		72,458

Engine

Std.	250-hp 351-ci 2-bbl. V-8
Opt.	290-hp 351-ci 4-bbl. V-8
	320-hp 390-ci 4-bbl. V-8
	335-hp 428-ci 4-bbl. V-8

1/4-mile (typical)

E.T.	14.6 secs.
Speed	99 mph

The Mach 1's base engine was a 250-horsepower 351 Windsor V-8 in 1969. The optional 335-horsepower 428 Cobra Jet V-8 (pictured) was accompanied by a Shaker hood and dual exhaust.

By 1969 the stakes and cubic inches had significantly increased in the musclecar wars. Ford responded with the Mach 1, which was available with 351, 390, and 428 V-8 powerplants. The high-performance package fastback featured a flat-black hood with racing-style pins, styled steel wheels, and tasteful graphics.

Mach 1 deck lids featured a subtle integrated spoiler lip, while the taillamp panel had a decal that outlined the panel. "Mach 1" bisected the stripe. Although not pictured, sport slats (louvers) and a deck lid spoiler were popular options.

higher, and who had "the right stuff" to pilot the air-craft to those new barriers.

A decade later, America was in the musclecar age and the buzz was about who could go quicker, faster, and who had the right stuff to pilot those street machines to record-setting runs.

In 1969, Ford had a Mustang for all reasons: economical six-cylinder models, models that excelled at road racing, models that were prime drag race equipment. And with the advent of the new Mach 1, Ford had what it believed was the right stuff—the ideal street Mustang.

The Mach 1 combined many of the best virtues of all the other Mustangs, which made it a truly exceptional car.

First, like the GT models, the Mach 1 had an elegant but racy appearance, inside and outside. The look was aggressive but understated, classy but subtle.

Borrowing from what it learned in road racing competition and in the development of the Trans-Am–inspired Boss 302, the Mach 1's "Competition" suspension system was tuned for precise handling on twisting, turning roads without a harsh, jarring ride.

Under the hood, Ford offered an assortment of engines, starting with the Mach 1's base 351 Windsor with two-barrel carburetion and 250 horsepower. Also available were a 351-4V rated at 290 horsepower and the 335-horse 428 Cobra Jet that was dominating drag races from coast to coast.

The 428 CJ was available in R-code form with a shaker-style hood scoop and Ram-Air induction, or the less obvious Q-code form, which had the same power rating but lacked the cold-air induction system. A third variant was possible: the Super Cobra Jet, or "SCJ" for short. Ironically, you couldn't just order the SCJ—you got it by default if you wanted either the 3.91:1 or 4.30:1 rear axle ratios. For the princely sum of $6.53 you got racing-style, heavy-duty connecting rods with cap-screw-style bolts; a unique crankshaft specifically machined for the LeMans-type rods; a flywheel and torsional vibration damper designed to work with the special crank and rods; and an engine oil cooler mounted ahead of the radiator. While the parts didn't add any power (at least according to Ford), they were worth their

weight in gold in terms of increased durability under the severe stresses of competition-type use.

Naturally, a Mach 1 could be ordered with a manual or automatic transmission, whichever the buyer preferred.

Finally—and perhaps most important—the Mach 1 was an exceptional value. For as little as $3,122, a buyer could drive away from the local Ford dealer in one of the most attractive Mustangs ever. And 72,458 buyers did just that in 1969, making the Mach 1 Mustang one of the most popular musclecars ever.

The Mach 1 name would soldier on through 1978, appearing on three different generations of Mustang by the time the plug was pulled. Although that longevity doesn't count for much, the original Mach 1's combination of prestige, handling, power, and pricing made it a milestone in the history of musclecars.

1969 Ford Torino Talladega

As the 1968 NASCAR season drew to a close, word of Dodge's secret weapon, the aerodynamic Charger 500, had already gotten out—and the competition was scared. Charger was already a fierce competitor, thanks largely to the Hemi engine.

1969 Ford Torino Talladega

Specifications

Body	Base Price	Units Built
Hdtp.	$3,680	754
Total		754

Engine

335-hp 428-ci 4-bbl. V-8 (Cobra Jet)

1/4-mile (typical)

ET	14.9 secs.
Speed	95 mph

The Torino Talladega was Ford's secret weapon in stock car racing competition during 1969. Aerodynamic principles were being effectively applied in NASCAR, and Ford had to compete against the winged Dodge Daytona Charger. The Talladega featured an aerodynamically sculpted nose extension and front bumper.

While the street versions of the Talladega were powered by the 335-horsepower 428 Cobra Jet, the race versions typically carried Boss 429s.

Production Talladega interiors were only slightly more comfortable than their race car counterparts'. A bench seat and column shifter were standard.

A sleek body would only make the Charger that much tougher to beat.

Upset that Chrysler wouldn't let him drive a Charger 500, long-time Plymouth driver and NASCAR superstar Richard Petty went shopping for a new ride. He wasn't about to finish as an "also-ran."

Ford was only too anxious to bring Petty on board. And they had just the car to offer him: the new Torino Talladega, which had been created in response to the Charger 500. With the Torino Talladega's fastbacklike rear end and its extended front end—which tapered slightly and used a modified Fairlane rear bumper on its front end to slice through the wind more easily—Petty knew he had found a car with the right stuff to compete against the wind-cheating Chargers.

And compete it did. Petty won his first outing in a Ford, at Richmond, and took 8 more firsts that season behind the wheel of a Talladega, along with a number of close second- and third-place finishes. Still, Petty finished second in points, after fellow Talladega driver David Pearson, who racked up 11 wins and 31 other top-five finishes.

Interestingly, the street Talladegas weren't available with the thundering Boss 429 powerplant that powered Petty's and Pearson's NASCAR racers. Instead, civilian buyers had to settle for a 335-horsepower 428 Cobra Jet. But that substitution vastly improved the street-driving characteristics of the Talladega, since the Boss '9 was notorious for its cantankerous nature and need for frequent tuning. The 428-CJ, on the other hand, was docile and torquey, day after day.

There was little else about the Torino Talladega that was well suited to daily driving. Its extended nose added some 6 inches to the car's length and made it more difficult to drive, especially when attempting to park. And visibility out the gently sloped rear window was poor, due to large blind spots created by the massive C-pillars. And if that wasn't enough to deter most buyers, the bare-bones interior made few friends. The Torino Talladega was built for speed, not comfort. If a part didn't help the Talladega go faster, it wasn't available on the car.

The "no-frills" mentality even carried over to the exterior identification of the car. Unlike its Mercury sibling, the Cyclone Spoiler II, which featured bold red and white or blue and white paint highlighted by either "Dan Gurney Special" or "Cale Yarborough Special" decals, the Talladega was available in traditional Torino colors with only three small "T" emblems to identify it—one on the top of each door, and another on the gas cap.

The Boss 302 wasn't your average Windsor-based 302. It was as close to a race engine as you could buy off the showroom floor. The 5-liter developed 290 high-strung ponies and featured a cross-drilled forged steel crank, forged steel connecting rods, forged aluminum pistons, four-bolt main bearing caps, and massive valve ports for maximum breathing.

Despite the Talladega's regular visits to Victory Lane, it wasn't tremendously popular with the buying public. NASCAR rules dictated that Ford had to sell at least 500 copies of the Talladega for the car to be legal for competition; at year's end, only 754 Talladegas had been assembled (plus an estimated 519 copies of the similar Spoiler II Mercury).

Still, the very fact that Ford went to such great lengths to create a car capable of dominating NASCAR racing makes the 1969 Torino Talladega a memorable piece of musclecar history.

1970 Ford Mustang Boss 302 & Boss 429

Ford was humiliated. Though the Mustang won the SCCA Trans-Am manufacturers' championship

Ford's desire to conquer the SCCA Trans-Am series spawned the Boss 302 Mustang. With the goal of winning the highly coveted road racing series, Ford pulled out all the stops to produce the best-handling car possible. The production car featured wide 60 series tires, large spindles, gusseted shock towers, 0.72-inch front sway bar, high-performance shocks, stiff springs, 16:1 steering ratio, and 11.3-inch disc brakes.

1970 Ford Mustang Boss 302

Specifications

Body

	Base Price	Units Built
Fastback	$3,720	7,013
Total		

Engine

290-hp 302-ci 4-bbl. V-8 (Boss 302)

1/4-mile (typical)

E.T.	14.8 secs.
Speed	96 mph

in 1967, it did so by a slim margin over the new kid on the block, Chevy's Camaro Z28. And the Z28 dominated the series in 1968, and again in 1969, winning the title both years. Things weren't much better in the world of NASCAR stock car racing, where Fords struggled for wins against the mighty Hemi Mopars.

Having wooed Bunkie Knudsen and Larry Shinoda from General Motors, Ford had inside information about the 1969 and 1970 Camaros long before they debuted. The Mustang engineering team put that knowledge to good use, refining the plans for its upcoming Mustangs to make them Camaro killers.

To reclaim the SCCA title, Ford built its own answer to the Z28—the Boss 302. In the past, Ford had relied upon Carroll Shelby's skunkworks facility to craft capable race cars. Shelby's GT-350 sported a number of modifications aimed at improving the

The Boss 429 Mustang had a dual role: homologate the Boss 429 semi-Hemi engine for use in NASCAR competition (even though Mustangs didn't race) and dominate drag racing.

Mustang's odds of winning on the track. While Shelby's Mustangs were fierce competitors on the track, their success failed to translate into the sales for which Ford had hoped because the cars were viewed as *Shelby*'s Mustangs, not Ford's.

Ford moved to correct this in 1968, by taking over production of the Shelby models. Yet even though Ford made no effort to conceal the fact that it was now building the Shelbys, the public still believed that Shelby was involved. Ford decided it needed an ultra-performance Mustang that was all its own.

For 1969, Shinoda gave them just what they were looking for in the Boss 302. With a completely reengineered 302 engine that featured a high-strength cylinder block, large-port heads, a race-ready cam, and other special touches, the Boss 302 had the pow-er to compete. Suspension, steering, and brake system upgrades gave it the agility to compete. And thanks to subtle, yet characteristic styling cues, the cars were highly recognizable whether at speed or in the winner's circle.

The Boss 302 wasn't an immediate on-track success, but it did garner its share of sales in the showrooms, which was ultimately more important to Ford. In 1970, when the modestly updated Boss 302 did dominate the sport, Ford was hardly upset about the publicity and image the wins brought.

NASCAR racing was a different matter altogether. Ford had a good reputation thanks to its numerous wins, but the company wasn't comfortable with competition being so equal. Simply put, the NASCAR Fords needed more power to outrun the

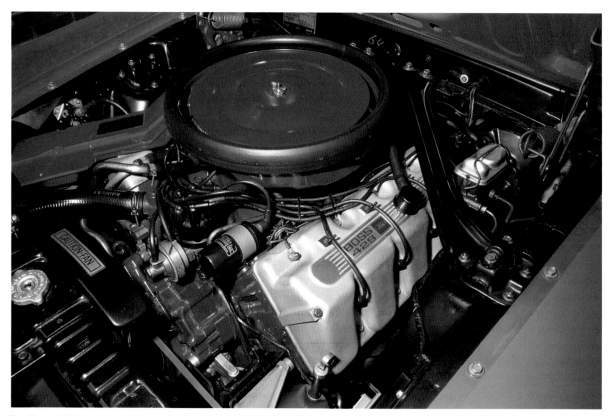

The Boss 429 featured massive aluminum cylinder heads with semi-hemispherical combustion chambers. The 375-horse engine's heads were so wide that the Mustang shock towers had to be reworked to make room for the engine, which was installed by Kar Kraft for Ford.

Mopars. That power came from a new 429-ci engine with massive cylinder heads cast with semi-hemispherical combustion chambers, similar to the Chrysler Hemi's. The Boss 429, as the engine was named, was built for the sole purpose of out-muscling the Hemi in NASCAR competition.

Designing and building the engine was a relatively easy task for Ford. The hard part was making sure it sold enough to homologate the engine for use in NASCAR racers. The company needed to sell at least 500, but the statisticians calculated it was unlikely that enough Torino buyers would shell out the extra $1,200 to put a radical engine—the Boss 429—under the hood. However, NASCAR didn't require an engine used for racing to be available in a vehicle used for racing. And since the odds said Mustang buyers would fork over the extra money for the burly Boss 429 engine, the decision was made to create a special, limited-production model called the Boss 429, after the engine.

Construction of the Boss 429 Mustangs, however, was a complex and expensive proposition—and one far too complicated to carry out on the regular production lines. So Ford contracted a Michigan specialty car company, Kar Kraft, to modify partially assembled 428 SCJ–equipped Mustangs to receive the massive Boss 429. Each Mustang's shock towers had to be cut and relocated 1 inch outward to make enough room for the Boss 429's huge cylinder heads, which made the engine nearly 2 inches wider than a 428 CJ. Unique control arms and spindles also dropped the front end roughly an inch to improve handling and appearance.

Externally, the Boss 429 contrasted sharply with its brazen Boss 302 little brother. The Boss 429 sported an attractive hood scoop with a manually operated cold-air induction system, a shallow air dam under the front lower valance, and unassuming "BOSS 429" outline decals—one per fender. Oh yes, and every Boss 429 received a small metal ID tag on the driver's door with the letters "KK" (for Kar Kraft) and the car's sequence number. Like Chevy's "COPO" Camaros, the Boss 429 was a true sleeper: It didn't look like much, but when asked to, it could trounce its competition without breaking a sweat.

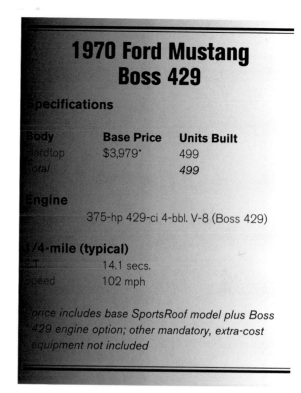

1970 Ford Mustang Boss 429

Specifications

Body	Base Price	Units Built
Hardtop	$3,979*	499
Total		499

Engine

375-hp 429-ci 4-bbl. V-8 (Boss 429)

1/4-mile (typical)

E.T.	14.1 secs.
Speed	102 mph

*price includes base SportsRoof model plus Boss 429 engine option; other mandatory, extra-cost equipment not included

As predicted, Ford had no trouble selling the required 500 units to legalize it for NASCAR use—859 units went down Kar Kraft's makeshift production line in 1969 and another 499 were built for 1970. Though it isn't entirely clear, it's generally believed Ford lost as much as $1,000 on every Boss 429 Mustang produced.

But the Boss 429 program was a success. The new engine—coupled with the Torino Talladega's sleek new nose—gave Ford's NASCAR race teams the muscle they needed to charge to the front, and stay there. Ultimately, Ford and Dodge battled quite evenly all season, nearly alternating wins from week to week.

Today, the Boss 302 and Boss 429 Mustangs are shining examples of how auto manufacturers could mass-produce race cars for the general public. Regardless of the ethical ramifications of such a move, history shows that the public eagerly received the Boss Mustangs, and their competition was most definitely intimidated.

Under the fiberglass hood breathed a standard Mustang 335-horsepower 428 Cobra Jet that gave the GT-500 potent power, but it was hardly as exotic as the modified Shelby engines of just a few years earlier.

1970 Shelby Mustang GT-500

Just five years after Ford had approached Carroll Shelby about producing special Mustangs in order to build a performance reputation for the Mustang, Shelby found himself disenchanted with his relationship with Ford. As Ford exercised more and more control over the development and production of the Mustangs that bore his name, Shelby became less and less satisfied with the results. It wasn't long before Shelby asked Ford to dissolve their partnership.

Confident that the Shelby project had accomplished its mission of establishing the Mustang as a respected performance car, Ford agreed to Shelby's request. In fact, Ford no longer needed Shelby to produce special Mustang models, as the company had an abundance of high-performance Mustangs in the lineup, including the GT, the Mach 1, the Boss 302, and the Boss 429—in addition to the Shelbys.

Though a Shelby in name only, the 428 Cobra Jet–powered 1970 Shelby GT-500 was still a formidable, as well as a very exclusive, musclecar. Special styling, interior, and powertrain changes set it apart in its final year of production. Only 789 GT-500s were released in 1970.

63

1970 Shelby GT-500 Mustang

Specifications

Body	Base Price	Units Built
Cp.	$4,709	
Conv.	$5,027	
Total		789*

Engine

335-hp 428-ci 4-bbl. V-8 (Cobra Jet)

1/4-mile (typical)

E.T.	14.6 secs.
Speed	99 mph

by-bodystyle breakdown is not available, and the 789 total units figure is disputable, though generally considered accurate

With so many exciting Mustangs to pick from, it's no wonder that buyers decided to choose from Ford's own, often less-expensive offerings. And while Ford had conservatively estimated there would be demand for roughly 4,000 1969 Shelbys, the company found itself with an estimated 789 of those cars still on-hand at the end of the 1969 model year.

Rather than sell the cars to dealers as leftovers (and thus at fire-sale prices), Ford chose to update the remaining cars and sell them as 1970 models at full price. As part of the update process, Ford replaced the identification tags on the leftover 1969s with 1970 tags, applied some black stripes on the hood and a Boss 302-like chin spoiler.

Again available in both GT-350 and GT-500 trim, the 1970 Shelbys were, essentially, Shelbys in name only. Under all that Shelby-specific bodywork—the fiberglass fenders with brake cooling ducts, the fiberglass hood with its three forward-facing and two rearward-facing NACA ducts, and the fiberglass deck lid and quarter-panel extensions—was mostly just typical Mustang mechanicals.

The GT-350's standard engine was the four-barrel–equipped 351 Windsor V-8, producing just 290 horsepower. Unlike previous Shelby engines, which featured extensive modifications, the 351W in the 1969–1970 Shelbys received only a high-rise aluminum four-barrel intake and aluminum Cobra valve covers.

GT-500s, such as the one pictured, continued to rely upon the 428 Cobra Jet big-block V-8 with its 335 horsepower and R-code cold-air induction, fed by the center, forward-facing hood scoop. Again, the cars were available with either a four-speed manual or three-speed automatic transmission. And the "Competition" suspension package featured the very same capable equipment found under Mach 1 models.

Likewise, the interior of the Shelbys was Deluxe Mustang fare, with the addition of a roll bar that not only improved the racy good looks of both the fastback and convertible models, but also added a degree of safety in the event the vehicle wound up with its wheels pointing skyward.

Although the 1969–1970 Shelby Mustangs were still plenty able to mix it up with Camaros, Firebirds, Challengers, and 'Cudas, they were hardly cut from the same cloth as the early, true Shelbys. But given the rarity and admirable performance of the 1970 Shelby Mustangs, those that survive today are highly prized treasures.

MERCURY DIVISION: FAST FORDS WITH HIGH FASHION

While Mercury's mission was to provide luxurious models at affordable prices, the company realized the importance of tapping into the burgeoning performance market. Apart from the additional sales and exposure, such a move would also help the company build brand loyalty among the young buyers in the hope of converting them into buyers of high-end (and highly profitable) luxury cars later in life.

Like its sister division, Ford, Mercury created a performance reputation the old fashioned way: by racing—and winning. Battles took place on drag strips and stock car ovals around the country.

Known more for its luxury, cars such as the 1969 Cougar Eliminator showcased Mercury's muscle-building talents. Larry Shinoda, who styled the Boss 302, developed the Eliminator package for Mercury. The semi-fastback, side stripes, and deck lid spoiler gave it a unique look.

Mercury built a limited run of Comets aimed at dominating drag strip competitions. A 289-powered model was cleared for competition in NHRA's B/FX class, and Mercury covered the A/FX class with Comets stuffed full of high-riser and SOHC 427s. Drag racing legends Dyno Don Nicholson, Eddie Schartman, and Hayden Proffitt all lit up the win lights in Mercurys; Dyno Don even did it in a Mercury Comet *station wagon*, which he believed had better weight transfer characteristics than the standard sedan—

something he credited for his 11-second class record and a season that saw only a single defeat.

And when it came to the NASCAR circuit, Comets—and later Cyclones—carried the Mercury name into Victory Lane. As the aero wars took center stage, Mercury was there with its Cyclone Spoiler and subsequent Cyclone Spoiler II.

Naturally, as word spread of Mercury's on-track accomplishments, its off-track business picked up, though never quite to levels that were completely commensurate with its finishes at the races. That meant that a significant portion of the buying public ended up missing out on the street versions of each of Mercury's racing models.

The buyers who didn't miss out were rewarded with cars that were every bit the equal of the more popular Ford performance models, but with more comfortable interiors and more stylized bodies. Mercury musclecars had the added advantage (for those buyers who valued it for some less-than-strictly-legal reasons) of not looking like musclecars nor did many people know much about their performance potential, so Mercury drivers had little trouble convincing unsuspecting victims to race them.

But when "performance" became a dirty word in the early 1970s, Mercury wisely refocused itself on the luxury car market. And though Mercury occasionally released performance cars throughout the remainder of the twentieth century—cars such as the imported Capri in the early 1970s, the 5.0-liter Mustang-based Capri of the 1980s, and the sporty Cougar at the turn of the century—its days of building musclecars were over. The surviving 1960s and 1970s Mercury musclecars have been left to preserve the memory of Mercury's hottest machines.

1969 Mercury Cougar Eliminator

An upscale Ford that's just right for taking down—or shaking down—the competition.

Despite all its market research, the various concept cars that were meant to test the waters, and the fact that the Mustang was going to be based on the Falcon underpinnings, the Mustang was still a huge financial risk for Ford Motor Company. Understandably, the company wasn't eager to let its Mercury division rush down a similar development path until the Mustang had proven itself.

Of course, following the sales stampede created by the 1965 Mustang debut in April 1964, there was little reason to hold back on plans for a Mercury pony car. In the fall of 1966 the Cougar hit showrooms featuring a number of refinements that differentiated it from the Mustang and uniquely qualified it as a Mercury, including softer suspension calibrations, a 3-inch wheelbase stretch, and of course the

Cougar Eliminators were available with a variety of engines, including the Boss 302 and base 351, but this particular 1969 model carried the legendary 428 Cobra Jet. With dual exhaust and a shaker hood, the 335-horsepower 428-powered Eliminator was a monster on the street.

unique front- and rearend treatments and other bodywork changes.

Though hardly the instant success that the Mustang was, the Cougars sold well—over 100,000 units a year during the first few years. For 1969 the Cougar was restyled and an exciting new performance model joined the line-up: the Eliminator.

The Eliminator, like Pontiac's GTO Judge, combined outstanding performance and a high measure of luxury with an unmistakable and aggressive appearance. Performance-wise, the Eliminator picked up where the previous year's GT model left off. Ride and handling were dictated by the Competition Suspension package, which offered taut handling without a jarring ride. More important to race fans were the engines, transmissions, and rear axle assemblies that were available—and there were several.

The base Eliminator engine was the 290-horse 351-4V, which was optionally available on Cougars. Up a step from that was the marginally more powerful Marauder 390 at 320 horsepower, or the Boss 302 with its 290 horsepower. The Cobra Jet 428 that appeared in late 1968 remained available, and for a very brief time the Boss 429 could be ordered, but

The Cougar's Mustang roots showed through inside, where the semi-cockpit-style instrument are obviously derived from the Mustang. A large analog tachometer and speedometer fed vital information to the pilot. Like other Ford products of the day, it featured the rim-blow steering wheel.

1969 Mercury Cougar Eliminator

Specifications

Body	Base Price	Units Built
Hdtp.	$3,979	2,200*
Total		2,200

Engine

Std.	300-hp 351-ci 4-bbl. V-8 (351C)
Opt.	290-hp 302-ci 4-bbl. V-8 (Boss 302)
	335-hp 428-ci 4-bbl. V-8 (428CJ)

1/4-mile (typical)

E.T.	15.8 secs.
Speed	90 mph

* 1,047 w/351C 1,047; 450 w/Boss 302 450; 444 w/428CJ

only if you had connections—just two found their way under Cougar hoods.

Buyers interested in a great *driving* car were wise to select the Boss 302, which was the very same high-winding engine that highlighted the Boss 302 Mustang. It was widely known that the Boss 302's 290 horsepower and equal torque ratings were greatly under-rated. Though a bit twitchy for around-town driving, the Boss 302—and, indeed, the Eliminator—was in its element blasting down twisting, curving roads.

On the other hand, buyers who were more into short jaunts of, say, a quarter-mile or so, were better served by the Cobra Jet 428. As with the Boss 302, the CJ's 335 horsepower rating was somewhat less than believable, especially given the durability built into the engine when delivered in Super Cobra Jet form, with its LeMans-style rods, heavy-duty crank, and other fortified components. The big-block 428 also made for an excellent street warrior, though it lacked the handling prowess that the smaller, lighter Boss 302 afforded.

As improved as the Eliminator was over a typical Mustang, and as competent as it was on the street and race tracks, it just never caught on with the public. Still, in spite of its May 8, 1969, intro date and little promotional fanfare, Mercury dealers had little trouble moving 2,411 copies of the Eliminator by the end of the 1969 model production in July. But a full year of production in 1970 actually saw a dip in sales to 2,200 units, with just under half getting the base 351 Cleveland engine and the other half split evenly between Boss 302 and 428CJ engines. Such low production numbers hardly justified the engineering, marketing, and sales efforts that Mercury poured into the car. But as unsuccessful as the Cougar Eliminator was sales-wise, it nonetheless stands as one of the ultimate—and rarest—Mercury musclecars.

CHAPTER 3

Chrysler Corporation

Big-Block Thunder and Small-Block Lightning

When you've got the King of Stock Car Racing, Richard Petty, in your camp, it's hard to fathom how you could be viewed as anything but serious about performance. And for Chrysler's Plymouth division, Petty was merely the icing on a multilayer performance cake.

Beginning in the 1950s, Plymouth was making a reputation for itself as a performance car company, thanks to such models as the Fury and engines such as the original Hemi.

Along came the 1960s and drag racing literally took off. When it did, Plymouth was right there with its Super Stock 413 and 426 cars that cleaned the clocks of nearly anyone who bothered to run against them.

King Richard held court over NASCAR racing with his Petty Blue Plymouths (except for 1969 when he temporarily jumped ship to race a Torino Talladega for Ford). For 1970 Plymouth was right in the thick of things with Petty at the wheel of its winged warrior, the Superbird.

Plymouths were regularly winning in one form of motorsports or another, and on the street. With such cars as the GTX, the Road Runner, and the legendary 'Cuda, Plymouth was able to earn its reputation every day of the week, often one stoplight at a time.

It's interesting to look back at each manufacturer's contributions to the musclecar era, to see what kind of mark each left. For Pontiac, it's clear that the GTO created the musclecar market. For Ford, it was the creation of the pony car market. Plymouth made the musclecar market fun. The Road Runner took its name from the popular cartoon character, and Plymouth played the connection for all it was worth by applying decals of the character to the car's exterior, interior, and even underhood. The company even gave the car a "beep-beep" horn. In 1970, when the end of the musclecar was on the horizon, Plymouth drenched its performance models in outlandish paint colors such as Panther Pink and Plum Crazy.

Plymouth's 1964 Sport Fury was purpose-built to wage war on drag strips, and it soon proved a formidable opponent on the street thanks largely to its Super Stock 426. The Wedge-head 426 with a single four-barrel carb and 10.3:1 compression ratio developed 365 horsepower at 4,800 rpms.

The Super Stock 426 big-block was not an engine for the timid: the "weak" S/S 426 put out 415 horsepower; the hot 426 put out 10 more horsepower. Note the dual-quad cross-ram intake and exotic exhaust manifolds.

1964 Plymouth Super Stock 426

Specifications

Body	Base Price	Units Built
Hdtp.	$3,379*	
Total		n/a

Engine		
Std.	415-hp 426-ci 4-bbl. V-8	
Opt.	425-hp 426-ci 4-bbl. V-8	

1/4-mile (typical)	
E.T.	13.1 secs.
Speed	112 mph

Today, it's a sad fact that the Plymouth nameplate is no more. But during the 1960s and 1970s no manufacturer was more into musclecars than Plymouth. The milestone musclecars on the following pages are proof of that.

1964 Plymouth Sport Fury

Chrysler was no stranger to the drag strip. Nor did it find building a high-powered drag car any kind of mystery. So when drag racing competition started heating up in the early 1960s, it was no surprise to find Chrysler continually leading the pack with its "Max Wedge" engines.

By 1964, with the competition breathing down its neck with 409 Impalas, "swiss-cheesed" Super Duty Pontiacs, and quick-as-lightning Thunderbolts, Chrysler instructed its engineers to find more speed for the company's Super Stock offerings.

Starting with the simple logic that bigger is better, the engineers hogged out the aging 413 engine and came up with an additional 13 cubic inches of displacement. A new, short-runner, cross-ram-style intake manifold improved the engine's ability to

breathe, while dual Carter four-barrels mixed fuel and air in ample volume. Two compression ratios were available with different power outputs—the "low" compression version used an 11.0:1 ratio that developed 415 horsepower, while the high-compression 13.5:1 engine made 10 additional horses. Regardless of compression, Chrysler gave the Super Stock engines an exotic exhaust system that consisted of unique, free-flowing, individual runner cast-iron exhaust manifolds, 3-inch head pipes with a crossover and dump tubes, and low-restriction twin mufflers for keeping things reasonably quiet on the street.

Behind the Super Stock 426 engine, buyers could select either a heavy-duty four-speed manual gearbox or Chrysler's fortified 727 TorqueFlite, which was generally considered to be the preferable equipment due to the highly consistent times it allowed, plus its cushioning effect, which extended the life of such driveline parts as universal joints, axle gears, and axles.

With huge power and a seriously upgraded suspension system, the Super Stock Sport Fury was capable of catapult-like launches with a high-G pull that just didn't quit until the driver lost his nerves or the road ended—either of which happened in a hurry. On the strip, stock S/S Sport Furys could run low-14s out of the box with inexperienced drivers at the wheel. Experienced drivers could rip off 13s until the cows came home. And with some tweaking and a few carefully selected aftermarket parts, including headers and slicks, mostly stock S/S Sport Furys were honest-to-goodness 12-second cars.

Apart from their bulletproof powertrains, the Sport Fury and its sibling, the Polara-based Super Stock Dodge, had a weight advantage compared to their usual competition. At 3,400 pounds, the Chrysler twins were the lightest cars in their class. When GM and Ford tried to even the scales by swapping in lightweight hoods, fenders, and bumpers, Chrysler responded in kind, dropping the Fury's weight to just over the 3,200-pound NHRA class minimum.

But the Plymouths (and Dodges) would likely have continued their winning ways without any exotic weight-loss programs. The cars were simply that good on the strip.

In the showroom, the Fury proved to be one of Plymouth's most attractive models ever—a

characteristic many Mopar enthusiasts still respect about the model. But even the non-Mopar-minded admit the Super Stock Sport Fury was an awesome performer—and a milestone of the times.

1967 Plymouth Belvedere GTX

When the automotive industry saw the public clamoring to get its hands on Pontiac's 1964 GTO, each manufacturer clamored on its own to catch up with Pontiac, and hopefully beat the GTO at its own game.

Plymouth's response to the GTO was the Belvedere, which evolved into the Belvedere GTX for 1967. The midsize Belvedere was a natural GTO combatant, with a similar size, weight, and general market.

But Plymouth had something that Pontiac couldn't compete with: an unlimited cubic-inch displacement policy. While GM hamstrung its intermediate models with a 400-ci cap, the Belvedere's designers had ready access to the Plymouth Super Commando 440, or the 426 Street Hemi.

For the performance-minded but cash-strapped, the 440 GTX was a bargain at $3,178 MSRP. Buyers got 375 horsepower, 480 foot-pounds of torque, a heavy-duty "Hemi" four-speed (or beefy TorqueFlite automatic), and a tough-as-nails 8 3/4-inch rear axle assembly. Armed with those items, the GTX more

The 1964 Sport Fury's interior was quite comfortable with bucket seats. Deluxe appointments included a console, a large-diameter steering wheel, and even a four-instrument gauge panel.

The GTX was fitted with the 375-horsepower Super Commando 440 V-8.

Standard GTX performance was provided by the 375-horsepower Super Commando 440, but the 425-horsepower 426 street Hemi was also available. At 3,545 pounds and 200.5 inches long, the GTX fit into the full-size musclecar category; but equipped with the killer 426 Hemi, it humbled most of its opponents.

This fully-appointed musclecar has bucket seats, console, rich carpeting, and a lot of chrome accents.

1967 Plymouth GTX

Specifications

Body	Base Price	Units Built
	$3,178	
	$3,418	
		12,690

Engine

375-hp 440-ci 4-bbl. V-8
425-hp 426-ci 2x4-bbl. V-8 (Hemi)

1/4-mile (typical)

14.6 secs.
96 mph

than matched any GTO's performance—and durability. But buyers who wanted to give a GTO no chance of keeping up could plunk down a couple hundred more dollars to equip their GTX with the mother of all performance engines: the awesome Street Hemi, which put 425 (under-rated) horsepower and 490 foot-pounds of torque at a driver's disposal—potential that Plymouth urged drivers to exercise with caution on the street.

With either engine, the GTX had what it took to win races—which it did in Top Stock Eliminator competition at the 1966 Springnationals, Winternationals, Summernationals, and World Championship Finals. With the Hemi, some fine-tuning, and a pair of slicks, a GTX could dash down the quarter-mile in the 11-second bracket.

The GTX also had what it took to win friends. Outside, GTX's styling was clean and classic, instantly attractive. Inside, it was simple but well appointed. No matter which way you sliced the GTX, it came up a winner.

Unfortunately, few Plymouth buyers recognized the GTX for the incredible buy that it was. By year's end, just 12,690 GTXes had rolled off Chrysler production lines, including 125 ultra-rare Hemi-powered units.

A year later, in 1968, the GTX found itself facing some serious competition from—of all places—Plymouth. When the new-for-'68 Road Runner hit the streets, it did so with bodywork identical to the GTX's—and a price that was $500 less. For most buyers, that savings more than offset the power difference between the Road Runner's 383 and the GTX's 440—and either could be had with the Hemi. A total of 44,599 Road Runners were sold—more than double the 18,940 GTXes that year.

GTX sales continued to dwindle in the coming years: 15,602 in 1969; 7,748 in 1970; and, finally, 2,942 in 1971. Even though the GTX never garnered huge sales, its performance record and its status as the big brother of the Road Runner preserve its seat at the musclecar table.

1970 Plymouth Superbird

If anyone doubted Chrysler's interest in winning NASCAR Grand National (now Winston Cup) races, they needed only a glimpse of the 1970 Plymouth Superbird.

From the Superbird's streamlined, wedge-shaped snout to its outrageous elevated rear wing,

Few cars make more of a statement than Plymouth's Road Runner–based Superbird. The front nose and rear wing created enormous downforce and gave the car a competitive advantage on NASCAR's high-speed ovals. Only 1,920 Superbirds were built for the street, making it one of the rarest Mopar musclecars ever made.

The Superbird's base engine was the 375-horsepower 440 Super Commando V-8, and the 425-horsepower street version of the 426 Hemi race engine was optional.

there was no mistaking the Superbird for grandma's grocery-getter. No sir, the Superbird was built for speed—and lots of it.

NASCAR's first round of "aero wars" kicked off in 1969, when Dodge debuted the Charger 500 and Ford countered with its Torino Talladega. Mercury got into the action with its Cyclone Spoiler II. And late in the year, Dodge pulled out all the stops and debuted its futuristic-looking Charger Daytona, on which the Superbird was based.

The Charger 500 had been Dodge's first attempt at improving the aerodynamics of its NASCAR star. The 500's flush-mounted grille and semi-fastback rear window boosted lap speeds by several miles per hour on NASCAR's superspeedways, and more important, proved there was much to be gained from improving the shape of a car.

Unfortunately for Dodge, Ford was a fast learner, and the Talladega (along with its Spoiler II cousin) was immediately competitive with the slick Dodge. Chrysler's engineers went back to the wind tunnel with scale models looking for more speed, and increased stability. They rightly reasoned that a wedge-shaped nose cone fitted to the Charger would have two distinct effects. First, it would slice through the air rather than bash against it. Second, properly

shaped, the aero nose would act much like an air foil, increasing downforce on the front end and helping to keep the front tires firmly planted during cornering.

But the Daytona's nose had an unexpected side effect: there was so much downforce on the front end that the rear of the car actually began to lift at speed, creating an incredibly loose handling condition. To restore stability, engineers experimented with a number of deck lid spoilers, but none generated enough rear downforce to counter the pressure on the front of the car. None, that is, until the engineers crafted an airplanelike wing and positioned it nearly 2 feet above the deck, between two massive supports. The height got the wing up into "clean" air, and the designers made the blade angle adjustable, allowing pit crews to tune the downforce for specific track conditions—more angle made more downforce, which was handy for shorter tracks, while big tracks required less blade angle.

Plymouth, which had been limping along at the races with its aerodynamic-as-a-brick Road Runner and GTX twins, had its engineers looking over the Dodge boys' shoulders during the aero and track tests of the Daytona. The Rapid Transit Authority then came up with some subtle enhancements for its

The Superbird measured 221 inches long and its wing was 24 inches high, 58 inches laterally across the back end, and 7.5 inches wide. It produced a maximum downforce of 600 pounds on the race track. The race version of the winged wonder was the first stock car to go over 200 miles per hour. The Superbird was so dominant in races that NASCAR banned the use of tall wings in 1971.

version of the winged wondercar, including a relocated and enlarged grille positioned on the underside of the nose, and slightly shorter rear wing supports to suit the needs of the Road Runner's roofline.

The Superbird was an immediate success, winning eight races during the 1970 season, while its less streamlined sibling, the Road Runner, racked up roughly another dozen victories on shorter tracks. Not a bad scorecard, considering Plymouth had only two wins during the previous year, both of which came before the Charger 500, Talladega, and Spoiler II debuted.

Bound by NASCAR rules, Plymouth had to offer the Superbird—complete with pointed proboscis and stratospheric spoiler—to the general public. As attention-getting as the aero devices were, they weren't exactly great street machines. The long nose made it hard to judge how close you were to cars ahead while parking or coming to a stop. The smallish grille limited cooling ability at street speeds. And the wing hampered rearward visibility, and even limited how far the trunk lid could open.

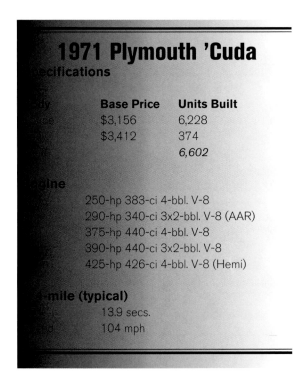

1971 Plymouth 'Cuda
Specifications

Body

	Base Price	Units Built
Coupe	$3,156	6,228
Conv.	$3,412	374
		6,602

Engine

250-hp 383-ci 4-bbl. V-8
290-hp 340-ci 3x2-bbl. V-8 (AAR)
375-hp 440-ci 4-bbl. V-8
390-hp 440-ci 3x2-bbl. V-8
425-hp 426-ci 4-bbl. V-8 (Hemi)

1/4-mile (typical)

13.9 secs.
104 mph

The Hemi was the ultimate Barracuda engine, but a variety of performance engines were available including the 335-horsepower 383 and the 390-horsepower 440 Wedge motors for the cost-conscious. A high-revving, triple two-barrel, 290-horsepower 340 was available in the AAR 'Cuda, which was Dodge's homologation special for Trans-Am road racing.

Despite their Road Runner roots, which gave the cars the necessary equipment to run well on the street—including standard 440 Super Commando or optional 426 Street Hemi power —Superbirds didn't exactly fly off dealers' lots. In total, some 1,800 were constructed and sold, many ultimately at deep discounts, just to get rid of them.

But the Superbird represented a definite high-water mark in musclecar aerodynamics—and it proved on race tracks that it had the muscle to put those sleek lines to good use. On those terms, no other musclecar even came close.

1971 Plymouth 'Cuda

When the Barracuda debuted in mid-1964, it was anything but a musclecar. But in true Ugly Duckling style, the Barracuda grew to become the envy of the musclecar market. Each year, Plymouth refined the Barracuda, transforming it from a Corvair- and Falcon-fighter to a fearsome Mustang- and Camaro-killer.

At no time was the 'Cuda—introduced in 1969 as a separate performance-oriented version of the Barracuda—more refined than 1971. When Plymouth first unleashed the 'Cuda option, it did so to address power shortcomings in the aging fastback Barracuda. In 1970, the Barracuda lineup was redesigned with a Camaro-esque long hood/short deck body that rippled with muscle.

For 1971, the one-year-old body was updated to smooth the design's few rough edges. Under the hood, the 'Cuda engine lineup was warmed-over from 1970 and most engines were re-rated to reflect the auto industry's move to the Society of Automotive Engineers (SAE) net horsepower ratings—which more realistically indicated how much power an engine would produce as installed in a production vehicle, rather than on an engine dynamometer. (Of course, any deliberate horsepower understatements by manufacturers in previous years still make comparisons tricky.) Otherwise, the 340, 383, both the four-barrel and six-barrel 440s, and the legendary Hemi were unchanged. GM and Ford made quick and drastic changes in their 1971 performance engine line-ups, making the 'Cudas appear all the more awesome.

Thanks to the chassis and suspension systems introduced in 1970, the 'Cuda continued to be one of the best-handling cars on the market, especially when equipped with the lightweight but plenty powerful 340 small-block engine, which produced a re-rated and still underrated 235 horsepower in 1971. Naturally, the straightline crowd was more attracted to the 440s and Hemis, but at $884 (plus the cost of the mandatory four-speed and other heavy-duty options) the elephant motor was a stretch for all but a lucky 115 'Cuda buyers—just 7 of whom went for their Hemi in a convertible body.

As exciting and powerful as the 1971 'Cuda was, there was still one area in which it couldn't compete with Camaros and Mustangs: sales. Those models sold more than 100,000 units each, whereas the entire Barracuda line didn't even account for 19,000 registrations that year—and just 6,602 were 'Cudas.

The following year, Chrysler detuned its musclecar program. The 'Cuda engine lineup was gutted. The only "performance" engine kept on the option list was the 340, which picked up 5 horsepower on

The Barracuda was first released in 1964, but the 1970 E-Body Barracuda joined the upper echelon of musclecars and was a genuine challenger to the Camaro and Mustang. With the exception of the Dart, the Barracuda was the lightest and smallest Mopar musclecar in 1970. When equipped with a Hemi, it became the fastest Mopar.

The short deck and long hood emulated the Mustang and Camaro, but the clean lines and distinctive styling were all Mopar. The 'Cuda featured a blacked-out taillamp panel and was available with a deck lid wing and rear window slats.

paper but was obviously far less powerful than the lower-rated 340 of 1971.

For the brief span of one model year, the 1971 'Cuda was the pinnacle of Chrysler musclecar creation, and for many today, the ultimate musclecar ever.

1971 Plymouth GTX

Chrysler was the last of The Big Three auto makers to respond to the government's and the insurance industry's pressure to scale back performance and exhaust emissions. While GM and Ford dramatically cut power for 1971—both in real terms through detuned engines, and on paper through a revised (net) horsepower rating system—Chrysler continued into 1971 as if the musclecar wars were still being waged.

One of Chrysler's last true musclecars was a descendent of one of its first—the Plymouth GTX. For 1971, the Satellite lineup—which included both the Road Runner and the GTX—was completely restyled with a new "fuselage"-style body that featured a long, low, wide look with a semi-fastback rear end treatment and a wraparound front bumper and recessed grille. Unlike the "slab" sides of the previous Belvedere body design, the new model had nicely sculpted sides with a strong feature line that separated the midsection from the lower body. The new shape proved as functional as it was fashionable when the King of Stock Car Racing, Richard Petty, was able to continue his winning ways behind the wheel of a 1971 Plymouth, conspicuously lacking GTX or Road Runner logos.

Inside, the cars were equally updated with all-new everything. Thoroughly modern—and even a bit futuristic—the new models were an immediate sensation in Plymouth dealerships, especially in two-door form. (Four-door models were actually remarkably different, sharing not a single body panel, and featuring a far more traditional, though similar, appearance.)

The same Super Commando 440 lurked beneath the curvaceous new sheet metal. A big revision to the power rating system dropped output to 330 *net* horsepower.

Under the GTX's new hood—which featured two simulated vents in standard form or a new, forward-facing, pop-up "Air-Grabber" cold-air induction system optionally—things were somewhat less than all new, which was a good thing in light of detuning by GM and Ford.

The GTX came with a re-rated version of the tried and true Super Commando 440, while the Road Runner continued to feature a 383 in exchange for a $600 savings. The 440, despite its new 305 SAE net horsepower rating, had yet to be castrated; it still had its high compression, its lopey cam, its large-port heads, and rich jetting in its Carter AFB four-barrel carb. As such, the GTX was one of the hottest performers of 1971, still able to rip off low-14-second passes with ease, while would-be challengers struggled to just break into the 14s.

In addition to the sleek new shape, new interior, and hot-as-ever engines, the 1971 GTX was the best-handling GTX to date, thanks to its extra-heavy-duty

The redesigned GTX received a contemporary long-hood, short-deck style, and a semi-fastback profile in 1971. The new body rippled with muscle and injected new life into the Mopar musclecar lineup.

The GTX's new, space-age interior was as attractive as the exterior and far more inviting than the previous generation's.

1971 Plymouth GTX

Specifications

Body	Base Price	Units Built
2-dr htp.	$3,733	2,942
Total		*2,942*

Engine

Std.	305-hp 440-ci 4-bbl. V-8
Opt.	330-hp 440-ci 3x2-bbl. V-8
	350-hp 426-ci 4-bbl. V-8 (Hemi)

1/4-mile (typical)

ET	14.8 secs.
Speed	94 mph

suspension system that was designed for more than just straightline acceleration. The brakes were also improved, which made the car a better—and safer—driving machine.

At year's end, however, fewer than 3,000 buyers saw fit to order a GTX, perhaps in part because of its $3,733 base price. The powers that be at Plymouth weren't impressed by the GTX production figures, and with the big 440 slated for extinction thanks to emissions regs, the GTX quietly disappeared from the product line.

DODGE: HAIL THE RAPID TRANSIT SYSTEM

It's almost a universal law that when you talk about musclecars, you have to at least mention a Dodge. The reasoning is simple: Dodge was so much a part of the musclecar movement that the two are practically inseparable.

Ironically, Dodge didn't have that many muscle-cars to hoot and holler about.

Sure, initially there were the Max Wedge Super Stock Dodges. Then in 1966 the Charger joined the lineup, and four years later the Dodge Boys finally joined the pony car race with its Challenger. There was also the Coronet, and the Super Bee. But by and large, there were few Dodge models aimed at the youthful musclecar market.

Perhaps the reason enthusiasts link Dodge so readily to the musclecar era isn't so much its cars, but the muscle behind them: Dodge's engines.

Though Chrysler Corporation shared the Dodge engines with the Chrysler and Plymouth lines, many enthusiasts think of the Hemi as a Dodge powerplant. And when they think of the beautiful (and powerful!) triple two-barrel setup on the RB big-block, they call it a "Six Pak"—Dodge's name for the system. (Heck, even Chevy fans call the Corvette Tri-Power setup a Six Pak!) And the 440 that the Six Pak comes on is generally called a "440 Magnum," even though that's just Dodge's name for it; Plymouth's 440 was the Super Commando.

Some have argued that Dodge's performance reputation was artificially inflated due to prominent roles in car movies such as *Bullitt, Vanishing Point,*

Dirty Larry, Crazy Mary, and even the TV series *The Dukes of Hazzard.*

But while the publicity no doubt helped solidify Dodge's reputation as a powerhouse, the company's accomplishments on race tracks left little doubt in anyone's mind about whether Dodge deserved its recognition as a musclecar maker. Dodge's Charger 500 was a terror on NASCAR's high-banked ovals in 1969. And less than a year later Dodge dropped the hammer on its NASCAR cruise missile, the winged and pointy-beaked Charger Daytona. Both were cars that sent the competition back to the trailers.

Like the Super Stock Dodges in the early part of the decade, the late-1960s and early-1970s Dodges did an outstanding job on drag strips, too, thanks largely to the mighty Hemi.

Dodge realized the importance of aerodynamics in stock car racing and attempted to harness the power of the wind with its sleek 1969 Charger 500's flush grille and semi-fastback rear window. With a 426 Hemi and 3.23 rear-end ratio, the automatic-equipped car sprinted through the quarter-mile at 14.01 seconds at about 100 miles per hour.

Whatever the reason, 1960s and early-1970s Dodges are known for their muscle. They were then, and they are today. A compilation of musclecar milestones wouldn't be complete without at least a few of the many deserving Dodges.

1969 Dodge Charger 500

While many musclecars were born to square off against a competitor in a battle of rapid acceleration, Dodge's 1969 Charger 500 was built for victory on the high-banked, high-speed ovals of NASCAR Grand National (now Winston Cup) racing. In fact, the "500" designation in the name represented the number of production units the company had to build to legalize the car for NASCAR competition—something the company did with only a handful to spare.

Starting with the B-body–based Charger from 1968, Dodge made the industry's first real science-based aerodynamic improvements to help the car achieve higher speeds. Two significant areas were addressed: Charger's standard, recessed grille; and the sail-panel roofline at the rear.

Replacing the recessed grille with a flush-mounted, Coronet-like grille minimized a major point of drag from the front end, and aided down-force that helped keep the front wheels firmly planted while cornering.

Charger's normal rear styling utilized two "flying buttress"-like sail panels, flanking a recessed rear window. The look was dramatic and exciting on the street, but the recessed window created a low-pressure zone that promoted aerodynamic lift of the rear end, destabilizing the car at high speeds. Complicating matters further, the massive sail panels acted like rudders in crosswinds, leading to some hair-raising rides for high-speed drivers.

The fix for the rear of the car was similar to that of the front: flush-mount the window with the peaks of the sail panels, creating a semi-fastback styling that smoothed the air stream over the car, allowing air to flow down the rear window, across the deck lid, and off the subtle lip at its rear edge. As it had with the front, removing the recessed area greatly enhanced downforce, and thus increased high-speed stability.

With the Charger 500's body capable of supporting sustained triple-digit speeds, racers finally had the ability to tap into the full power of Dodge's

While the Charger 500's body was designed to slice through the wind, the already-legendary 426 Hemi was designed to suck in gobs of it and convert it to race-winning horsepower—425 horsepower in street trim.

Charger interiors were among the finest available. Bucket seats were both comfortable and supportive, while six gauges in the instrument panel kept a driver well informed of the machine's status.

engines—namely, the 440-ci, Wedge-"B-motor" and the legendary 426 Hemi. The latter was available to the public in 425-horsepower "Street Hemi" form.

The Mighty Mopars proved to be formidable opponents, especially with driver Bobby Isaac at the wheel of the K&K Insurance–sponsored 1969 Charger, which won nearly half of the races that season. And the effectiveness of the aerodynamic alterations wasn't lost on the competition; Ford and Mercury each took their high-bank warriors to the wind tunnels and developed unique front-end treatments for them, creating the Torino Talladega and the Cyclone Spoiler II. General Motors, which had only unofficial participation in NASCAR racing at the time, passed on the investment necessary to streamline its eligible models.

The Charger 500 showed Chrysler—and the automotive world—that aerodynamics was every bit as important as engine power. The company would hammer the point home the following year with its radical pair of "winged warriors," the Charger Daytona and Plymouth Superbird. Their pointed nose cones and 3-foot-tall, adjustable deck lid spoilers produced incredible downforce, allowing the cars to run at more than 220 miles per hour during testing at the 2.6-mile Talladega Superspeedway—well beyond the safe limits of the day's tire technology.

But the Charger 500 had impact far beyond the musclecar wars and the high-banked battles. Years later auto manufacturers would incorporate some of the lessons learned from the Charger 500 and the later wing cars into everyday production vehicles, not for high-speed performance but rather highway-speed fuel economy. Rarely can a musclecar lay claim to improving fuel mileage, but the Charger 500 can.

In the end, the Charger 500 was a one-year-only model that drew barely enough buyers to qualify it for competition use; the general public knew little, if anything, about it. Yet because of its aerodynamics, the Charger 500 has had a lasting effect on nearly every car buyer since, making it a noteworthy combatant in the musclecar wars.

The recessed grille on standard Chargers acted like a parachute, slowing the cars, but the 500's flush Coronet-like grille prevented that and was responsible for a noticeable increase in speed of several miles per hour, depending on the track. The "500" indicated the number of Charger 500s Dodge built—the very same number NASCAR required in order for the car to be legal for competition use.

1969 Dodge Charger 500

Specifications

Body	Base Price	Units Built
Hdtp.	$3,860	500
Total		500

Engine

Std.	375-hp 440-ci 4-bbl. V-8
Opt.	425-hp 426-ci 2x4-bbl. V-8 (Hemi)

1/4-mile (typical)

E.T.	13.9 secs.
Speed	104 mph

CHAPTER 4

American Motors Corporation

Bold, Brash, and Eclectic

Mention "American Motors" to most Americans old enough to remember the company and the first image that usually pops into their minds is the Pacer — or the Gremlin. But musclecar enthusiasts don't think like most people. Maybe that's why they tend to remember AMC's successes, rather than those two arguable failures.

AMC intially denounced other auto manufacturer's involvement in the marketing of performance cars, and lost a lot of ground in doing so. When the company realized that performance was what the buying public wanted, it threw all its engineering, marketing, and executive weight behind its own performance programs. A light had gone on at the top of the company, with AMC suddenly convinced that it needed its own contenders on the street and the race track. Of course, many believe that AMC's very survival *did* depend on it succeeding in the musclecar market. And amazingly enough, AMC made remarkable progress in a very short time.

The company's first effort was a slightly souped-up Rambler. The following year, the Rambler was upgraded with a 343-ci V-8 that really caught people's attention. In 1969—with George Hurst's help—AMC unveiled the SC/Rambler, complete with a 315-horse 390 under the hood, making the car more than a match for any Chevy II/Nova, even if its styling was a little dated by then.

Despite running a distant fourth (of four) in sales and size, AMC led the way in several performance markets. The AMX, which stood for American Motors eXperimental, was a two-seat personal sports car along the lines of the 1950s Ford Thunderbirds. Wielding 390 power, impressive handling, dynamite styling, and comfort to boot, the AMX was a delightful performance car.

AMC's answer to the Chevy II/Nova SS was the SC/Rambler, which it codeveloped with shifter mogul George Hurst. Just 1,512 units were produced, including 1,012 with this "A" paint scheme. Along with the potent 390, the SC/Rambler featured a torque-linked rear axle, front disc brakes, AMC/Warner Gear T-10 four-speed with heavy-duty clutch, and a Model 20 rear axle.

The enormous and fully functional Ram-Air hood scoop helped boost horsepower and pushed the car to 14.3 seconds at 100.8 miles per hour.

The AMX's big brother, the Javelin, was another sure thing, thanks to its outstanding styling, thrilling performance, and exceptional value.

AMC didn't just build these cars for the street and claim they performed—they took the cars racing. Out on the track, the little AMCs were equally impressive. The Javelin faired well in SCCA Trans-Am competition right from its first race, and won the manufacturers' championship in both 1970 and 1971. In drag racing, AMX and Rambler models—and later, Gremlins—were fairly common sights and were rarely defeated easily.

But the one venue in which AMC had the most difficulty succeeding was the most important one: dealers' showrooms. No matter what AMC did to improve its image, no matter how many races it won, no matter how great its new cars were, and no matter how "catchy" its advertising campaigns, the public just wasn't buying enough AMC models to keep the company afloat.

Today, surviving AMC models such as the AMX, the Javelin, the Rebel Machine, the SC/Rambler, and others are bold reminders that tiny AMC once took on the big boys on the streets and strips of America—and won.

1969 1/2 AMC/Hurst SC/Rambler

Little AMC was doing its best in 1969 to catch up to the Joneses—The Big Three Joneses. The company had publicly stated in 1964 that it would have nothing to do with the performance wars being staged between GM, Ford, and Chrysler. But with sales projections growing bleaker by the day, the company was forced to take drastic action or suffer the consequences.

The company realized that passing on the performance car market just didn't make sound financial sense, so in 1965 it began working on a number of projects aimed at creating a performance image.

By 1969, AMC blasted onto the racing scene with a vengeance. It was running Javelins in SCCA Trans-Am competition, and with the help of George Hurst (the Hurst in "Hurst Shifters") the AMX was doing damage in professional drag racing. While the company was working on street versions of the Javelin Trans-Am and the AMX drag car, both of those were largely competitors for pony cars such as the Camaro and Mustang. That left AMC absent from a number of performance car markets.

Although the company hadn't yet formulated a strategy for competing with other makers' midsize and full-size musclecars, the company did have something for the compact-car market.

The Rambler American was AMC's answer to Chevy's Chevy II (later renamed Nova) and Ford's Falcon. But those models were soon uprated. Ford's performance Falcon was something called the Mustang (the two shared a common platform), and Chevy created the Nova Super Sport and stuffed its engine bay with a hot 327-ci V-8. AMC initially responded with the 1966 1/2 Rogue, but the Rogue's 225-horse 290 V-8 proved to be no match for the Chevy 327 or the Mustang's hi-po 289.

A year later, AMC rolled out the 1967 1/2 Super-Americans, which evened the score somewhat, thanks to the 280-horsepower 343 V-8. The Super-Americans were good, but they had their problems.

When AMC got the idea to redo the Super-American for 1969, they asked George Hurst to apply to the Rambler some of what he learned prepping 53 AMXes for Super Stock duty. The cars he created were the Hurst SC/Ramblers—the "SC" stood for "SuperCar."

The first course of action was to improve the SC/Rambler's engine. The trusty 343 was ousted in favor of the AMX 390 with its 315 horsepower. Curing one of the factory limitations of the Super-Americans, AMC installed a factory dual-exhaust system fitted with Thrush glasspack mufflers.

Chassis flex had been a common complaint about the Super-Americans, to such a degree that tales of broken windshields weren't uncommon. Things would only get worse with the 390's boosted torque. To remedy the problem, the SC/Rambler chassis was reinforced at key structural points.

The 390 was linked to a T-10 four-speed via a heavy-duty clutch, and a T-handle Hurst shifter (of course) poked through the floorboards. Out back, the AMC Model 20 rear axle assembly was fitted with 3.54:1 gears and a Twin-Grip limited-slip differential, while AMX Torque Links were reengineered to fit the American chassis to control wheel hop and aid handling. Front disc brakes were made standard to haul the car down from speed safely and swiftly.

To make sure an SC/Rambler wasn't mistaken for a garden-variety, little ol' lady's Rambler, the car was given flamboyant red and blue accents. Initially, the SC/Rambler paint scheme consisted of massive red side stripes, blue graphics on the hood, and blue Magnum 500–styled steel wheels with redline tires. A fiberglass hood sported a boxlike scoop that angled upward to ingest cold air as it rushed over the car, and a huge blue arrow pointed into the scoop with red "390 CU.IN." bisecting the arrow's head from its stem. AMC built 500 SC/Ramblers with this paint scheme, then revised it with a more subdued "B" paint appearance. It was still a white car, but the B version did away with the huge red sides in favor of a much narrower, 2-inch red lower body stripe above blue rocker areas. The hood also lost the bold graphics, though it did retain the hood pins and cables. Five hundred "B" cars were built. When those were sold, a third batch consisting of 512 SC/Ramblers was built with the original "A" paint scheme, for a total of 1,512 SC/Ramblers.

Regardless of the paint treatment, all the SC/Ramblers were the same inside (and in every other respect, since there were no options). Each car featured gray vinyl front seats that weren't buckets but were more like individual minibenches. The seats, which had red, white, and blue-striped headrests, were too close together for a console or even an armrest. A wood, three-spoke steering wheel gave orders to the front wheels, while a standard Rambler dash was jazzed up only slightly with a Sun tach that was secured to the steering column with a stainless-steel hose clamp.

The SC/Ramblers were fearsome on the streets or the track, thanks to their envious power-to-weight ratio. And at the SC/Rambler's $2,998 sticker price, it was one of the best bargains of the musclecar era—especially given its ability to blast down the quarter-mile in just 14.1 seconds as it did for *Road Test* magazine's testers.

The one-year-only SC/Rambler was, indeed, a match for its competition—and just about any other car it could come across on the streets. But, once again, despite building a better mousetrap, AMC just couldn't sell enough cars to make the SC/Rambler a

1969 AMC Hurst SC/Rambler

Specifications

Body	Base Price	Units Built
Hdtp.	$2,998	1,512
Total		1,512

Engine

315-hp 390-ci 4-bbl. V-8

1/4-mile (typical)

E.T.	14.2 secs.
Speed	100 mph

worthwhile venture. Besides, the Rambler was in its last year of production, with the new Hornet waiting in the wings to replace it.

1969 AMC AMX California 500 Special

American Motors wasn't exactly known for building performance cars in the 1960s. After all, AMC—the company formerly known as Nash—brought us the Rambler and the Metropolitan, which were successful if a bit plain, as well as the Gremlin and the Pacer, which have the dubious honor of having been voted two of the ugliest cars ever by *Car & Driver* readers.

Credentials such as those are, perhaps, what make AMC success stories—the AMX—so interesting.

The AMX grew out of the 1965 skunkworks Project IV program, which created four concept cars: the AMX, the AMX II, the Cavalier, and the Vixen. While the Cavalier and Vixen were more mundane in nature, the AMX and AMX II were designed with sportiness in mind. The AMX show car was styled as a 2+2 with a unique "Ramble" (in homage to the company's Rambler models) seat in place of a trunk. When show crowds voiced strong interest in the AMX's attractive styling, the company quickly enlisted the talents of Italian metalworkers at Vignale to construct a functioning AMX prototype.

When the Vignale AMX joined the Project IV tour, reaction became even stronger, and the AMX was fast-tracked for production—with a few select changes. Wiser heads prevailed and nixed the Ramble seat to avoid potential legal troubles, and, in fact, the 2+2 seating configuration was killed entirely. Fortunately, deletion of the Ramble seat had little effect on the AMX's attractive profile. To cut production costs, the AMX was engineered to ride on a shortened Javelin chassis.

The 1968 AMX styling was perfect for competing with the recently redesigned Mustang and the GM pony car twins, the Chevy Camaro and Pontiac Firebird. The AMX's long hood with simulated, side-facing vents, attractively sculpted sides, and a fastback rear end and massive, muscular C-pillars was sporty, yet tough.

Had it not been for another AMC skunkworks project, those looks would have been only skin deep. Fortunately, the company's all-new 290 was an economical base engine, whose 343- and 390-ci versions proved to be capable performance engines, serving up 280 and 315 horsepower, respectively. The beauty of the AMC 290/343/390 engine was that it produced big-block power without traditional big-block bulk and heft. Weighing in under 600 pounds, the engines compared quite favorably to the big-blocks offered by the Big Three, which tipped the scales anywhere from 750 to 850 pounds. Though the AMC engine may have been down a bit on power, compared to the Chevy 396, Ford's 428, or Chrysler's 426 Hemi, its power-to-weight ratio made it a good competitor and gave the AMX better handling capabilities since it had less weight over the front wheels.

Of course, in the 1960s, the measure of a musclecar was its quarter-mile elapsed time. Even here, the AMX could run with the big boys, with box-stock runs of 14.3 seconds. Still, AMX trap speeds of

With the AMX's 315-horse 390, the SC/Rambler was serious competition for the Chevy Nova and Dodge Dart. With a number of Group 19 (AMC high-performance) parts, the SC/Rambler could run in the mid- to low 12s.

AMC cars had a personality all their own. Other than the Corvette, the AMX was the only two-seat musclecar of the era. This 1969 AMX California 500 Special wears Trendsetter Sidewinder sidepipes, and special brass plaques on the hood blisters identify it as a 500 Special.

The AMX's base engine was a 290-ci V-8, but a 343, 360, and the stellar 390 V-8 were also available. The 390 had a 4.17 by 3.57-inch bore and stroke and pumped out 315 horsepower.

AMX interiors had a look similar to that of the 1969 Mustang, thanks to the twin-cockpit design. The short-wheelbase muscle/sports car featured large, easy-to-read analog gauges, bucket seats, and a floor shifter for both automatic and manual transmissions.

94 miles per hour indicated a horsepower shortage compared to its competition, which often ended the quarter-mile dash at better than 97 miles per hour.

A tasteful appearance and good performance were often enough to win buyers, but AMC could not afford to take chances. An inviting interior was fitted between the doors, though one accommodated just two occupants. Richly upholstered bucket seats plus stylish door panels and a simple, yet pleasing instrument panel and dash kept a driver and passenger comfortable, informed, and in control of an AMX at any speed.

By all respects, the AMX was a fine piece of work, and AMC had every reason to be proud. But the competition had the upper hand on the sales floor. In its first year, 1968, dealers sold just 6,725 AMX models. In the following 12 months, they put through orders for 8,293. But for the model's third and final year, a mere 4,116 were constructed.

Fortunately for AMC, the AMX was never purely about generating impressive sales figures. To be sure, that would have been a delightful coincidence. In truth the AMX was as much about drawing buyers to AMC dealerships as it was about its own sales figures. In that respect, the AMX was a quantifiable

1969 AMC AMX California 500

Specifications

Body	Base Price	Units Built
Hdtp.	$3,297	8,293
Total		8,293*

Engine

315-hp 390-ci 4-bbl. V-8

1/4-mile (typical)

E.T.	14.6 secs.
Speed	96 mph

*includes: 284 "Big Bad Orange"; 195 "Big Bad Blue"; and 283 "Big Bad Green"

success, and many enthusiasts credit the car—for a while, at least—with changing the outlook for a foundering AMC. Keeping a sinking corporation afloat is something few musclecars can lay claim to.

1970 AMC Javelin Trans-Am

Since its introduction in 1968, AMC's Javelin had been steadily improved, both in appearance and performance. The press had given the car rave reviews, especially in comparison articles in which the Javelin was pitted against Camaros, Mustangs, and other pony cars.

The Javelin had sold well—more than 50,000 units in 1968, and 40,000 in 1969—but still wasn't a smashing success in the performance car market.

Having returned to profitability in 1969, AMC was convinced it had rounded a corner and was on its way to a profitable recovery. So the notion of spending a bunch of money on a bona fide racing program wasn't nearly as far-fetched as it had been when money was considerably tighter.

AMC didn't kid itself. It knew it couldn't feasibly compete in organized drag racing or stock car racing, where engineering and cost demands knew no bounds. The SCCA's Trans-Am series offered high visibility and better odds of winning events. With these prospects on the horizon, AMC launched an all-out assault on the Trans-Am series with the goal of capturing the manufacturers' championship.

There was only one problem: AMC didn't have the know-how to field competitive cars. The solution to this dilemma was to contract Roger Penske's organization to field Javelins. Penske's shops built the cars and SCCA pro Mark Donahue drove them. Together, the pair was almost unstoppable. After early development pains, the Javelins eventually succeeded in taking home 5 first-place trophies, of the 11

awarded that season. (Donahue would do even better in 1971, scoring the first win of the season, plus six more in a row to take seven of the first nine events—and the manufacturers' championship.)

AMC wasted no time in capitalizing on its performances in Trans-Am racing. Ads—some of the boldest of the entire musclecar era—screamed "From zero to Donahue in 3.1 years" and "Donahue puts his mark on the Javelin." Another interesting ad showed a race-ready Javelin and a 1970 Javelin side by side and told of the virtues of "A Javelin for the track. A Javelin for the road."

The Javelin for the road was one of the 100 Javelin Trans-Ams assembled to homologate the car for Trans-Am competition. Each of the 100 were mandatorily painted in a bold and patriotic red-white-blue hash paint scheme. Also standard was the 315-horse 390 engine, dual exhaust, a limited-slip differential, a Hurst-shifter four-speed, front disc brakes, heavy-duty springs and shocks, front and rear

AMC's performance workhorse, the 390 V-8, was the Javelin's top engine option. Due to the added weight and size, the Javelin posted slower quarter-mile times than the AMX. Still, the 315-horse 390 pushed the Javelin to 15-second E.T.s in the low-90-mile-per-hour range, which weren't too shabby.

AMC and Penske Racing selected the Javelin for use in SCCA Trans-Am competition and handily won the championship. This 1970 Javelin's wild red, white, and blue paint scheme celebrated its racing accomplishments.

The Javelin instrument panel featured a clock on the far left, a huge speedometer in the middle, and an equally large tachometer on the right. A Hurst T-handle shifter was mated to a four-speed Warner Gear T-10 transmission.

spoilers, fat F70x14 tires, and a 140-mile-per-hour speedo plus a tach to keep tabs on the engine.

The outrageously painted Javelin Trans-Ams drew throngs of fans and speed freaks to AMC dealers. Yet, while an interesting curiousity, few inspired buyers to plunk down money for the unique appearance. But eventually, the 100 models were sold, legalizing the car for competition—or so AMC thought.

Before the start of the 1970 racing season, the SCCA changed the Trans-Am homologation rules. Instead of just 100 models, AMC now had to sell a total of 2,500! Realizing buyers wouldn't possibly buy 2,400 more copies of the tricolor Javelins, AMC quickly decided to make better use of its association with Roger Penske and, especially, Mark Donahue. The Javelin Trans-Am package was changed; it now came in any standard Javelin color, and it was renamed the Mark Donahue Special 1970 Javelin. Donahue's signature was written on the rear of the deck lid spoiler that he helped design, based on the one he used on his race car. The car proved much more popular—even in flamboyant colors such as

Big Bad Orange, Big Bad Green, or Big Bad Blue—and AMC handily sold 2,501 Donahue specials.

The very fact that AMC funneled so much effort and expense into a performance program at a time when the company was literally on the verge of collapse is remarkable and showed AMC commitment to establishing itself as a respected player in the performance car market. But despite all the money, despite all the race wins, and despite the Javelin's rave reviews and the fact that it proved to be a formidable competitor on the streets and race tracks of America, the Javelin just wasn't what enough buyers were looking for.

AMC continued its support of Trans-Am racing in 1971, extending its backing to a second team, Roy Woods Racing. But with Ford, GM, and Chrysler officially out of Trans-Am, the competition was minimal and AMC won the manufacturers' crown with almost no effort. Per its contract with Penske, AMC continued its support for 1972, but promptly pulled the plug on its Trans-Am adventures at the end of the season, despite winning its second straight manufacturers' championship. Two years later, the Javelin drifted off into obscurity, and a few years later, so did AMC.

1970 AMC Javelin Trans-Am

Specifications

Body	Base Price	Units Built
Hdtp.	$3,995	100
Total		*100*

Engine

325-hp 390-ci 4-bbl. V-8

1/4-mile (typical)

E.T.	15.1 secs.
Speed	91 mph

INDEX